LUCKY CODE

A GUIDE FOR WINNING AT LIFE

by Gayneté Edwards

Acknowledgements

Book designer: Duane Jones of Be Glitterati
www.beglitterati.com

Editor: Amy Scott of Nomad Editorial
www.nomadeditorial.com

For media or print interviews with Gayneté:
contact@gaynete.com

Copyright © 2015 by Gayneté Edwards

All rights reserved. This book or any portion thereof may not be reproduced or used in any manner whatsoever without the express written permission of the publisher except for the use of brief quotations in a book review.

Printed in the United States of America
First Printing, 2015
ISBN 978-1-927750-87-2

This book is dedicated to my sweet hazel-eyed little girl, Ramaya.
May the infinite sky be your limit always!
xoxo

CONTENTS

Introduction	VII
Code A: Accept the Good That Comes Your Way	1
Code B: Blame Game—Choose to Sit Out!	7
Code C: Character Building	13
Code D: Dress for Success	19
Code E: Eliminate the Negativity	25
Code F: Free Yourself from Mind Clutter	35
Code G: Give Graciously	41
Code H: Hobby—Get a Good One!	47
Code I: Indebtedness—Just a Fancy Word for Gratitude	53
Code J: Joke Is on You	59
Code K: Know When to Let Go	65
Code L: Listen to Your Heart	71
Code M: Mentors Are a Power Source	77
Code N: Network... Then Network Some More	87
Code O: Own Your Truth	95

Code P: Prayer and Support Teams—Do Not Skip This One!	**101**
Code Q: Question Yourself Daily	**107**
Code R: Roll Up Your Sleeves	**113**
Code S: Surround Yourself in Solitude	**119**
Code T: Time to Cut Fear	**127**
Code U: Use Your Resources	**133**
Code V: Victory Perspective—Take This View	**139**
Code W: Winning Plans of Purpose	**147**
Code X: Jump Hurdles (Case in Point)	**155**
Code Y: Yes Men Quickly Become Trash Cans	**161**
Code Z: Zero to Hero? Remain Humble	**167**
Luckieville Wrap-Up	**173**
The Luckie Decree	**175**
Resources: Because Sharing Is Caring!	**177**

INTRODUCTION

Raffles. Scratch cards. Slot machines. Contests. Bets. I win them quite often. Privileged "coincidences"? I have them *all* the time (we will get into the juicy details behind some of these winnings a little later). I am fortunate and quite content with the life I live. Contrary to popular belief, however, there is no mystical rainbow following me around everywhere I go. Nor did my ancestors pass on some "lucky" gene.

Let's briefly take a look at the word *luck*. Dictionary.com defines it as "a combination of circumstances, events, etc., operating by chance to bring good or ill to a person." I suggest you dismiss right now the idea that all of your circumstances arise "by chance." It's rubbish. In fact, the whole concept of "luck" and how it is attained is rubbish—yup, you have been tricked. I don't know about you, but I for one like to have a reasonable amount of control over what happens to me. Of course, we have all experienced terrible circumstances at one point or another that we have felt that we had no control over. The good news is that how fast we rebound, and what we choose to do next, are on us. To bring positive change to our circumstances, we must first commit to changing ourselves. All that we are, and all that we can be, begins with us. Our thoughts and our actions—both of which we have complete control over—shape the course of our lives and our "luck."

I have always been identified as the ridiculously lucky one, but that's not by chance; it's because I strategically set myself up to be lucky—no rabbit foot, horseshoe, or four-leaf clover required, just good old-fashioned dedication to following a few basic codes. Those codes, which are outlined here in this book, have been tried and tested by myself and my lucky friends. I like to call us "Luckies"—we're the ones whom everyone else calls lucky, but we know the truth: we create our own luck. I hope that by the end of this book you will commit to joining us in Luckieville by using a few (or all) of the codes found within to change your luck in life on a daily basis.

If you're anything like me, you believe that your time is a precious commodity and you don't want to waste it. I respect that, and as such, have taken a no-frills approach with this book. I get to the meat and potatoes of what you need to do to get lucky, without the fluff. Now with expectations managed and intentions clear, let us continue.

I do not believe in "lucky coincidences" (hence why the words are always in quotation marks). You bought this book for a reason. Yup, we were meant to find each other, and I would like to assist you on your life's journey in any way I possibly can. We can keep in touch long after you finish reading at www.gaynete.com. I want to hear all about how these codes change your life; I have every confidence that they will, if you commit to using them regularly.

Stop reading right this moment, however, if you believe that you have no flaws and you have all of the answers. This book is not for the perfect person, but for everyone else. It is for those who see good things happening all around them and feel that they cannot catch a break. For the individuals who truly want to be a better version of themselves. For those who aren't quite sure what they want, but do know that they want something a little better than what they currently have. It is also for those who are already winning at life and want a refresher course or some extra tips to become even greater. If you have made it this far, congratulations—your journey to Luckieville awaits.

CODE A

Accept the Good That Comes Your Way

Of all the codes, the first may be the hardest: we must accept the good that comes to us. We have been subconsciously taught to shy away from compliments and to play down our victories. We've been told that to do otherwise comes across as vain and demonstrates an inflated ego. This is simply not the truth. In fact, by rejecting the good, we are pushing more instances of good further and further away, unconsciously sending a message that we do not want any more of it. The sooner we realize this and begin accepting the good things that come our way, the better our happenstances.

As with everything in life, there are extremes, and one can come across as egotistical if this is taken too far, but that's not what I'm talking about here. I am referring to a simple "thank you" after receiving a compliment, rather than dismissing or deflecting it with comments like, "These old things?" or "Please—yours are way better." I know this sounds familiar and that we have all been guilty of this before. The key is to move forward and to be aware the next time around.

Simply appreciating something given to you (whether it be a compliment or the newest iPhone won in a contest), rather than downplaying or finding something wrong with it in an effort to disguise how special it felt for you to receive it, assists to attract more of the good in the future and helps you to feel a lot better in the process. Negativity slows down your journey to Luckieville, so avoid it at all costs. We'll discuss negativity in greater detail later (if you want to jump ahead, see Code E: Eliminate the Negativity).

As simple as Code A appears, it is a difficult one to master when we are not used to responding in this way. But all hope is not lost! We are on a mission to get lucky in life, and are willing to put in a bit of effort in the process, right? There is a reason that so few people have this thing we call "luck." It requires a constant tweaking of our current codes that have been embedded for decades. It is a lifelong process, but do not be discouraged, because it doesn't take that long to begin reaping the benefits. The better you get at accepting the good, the luckier you will be.

How to Apply Code A:
Accept the Good That Comes Your Way in Daily Life

The next time you receive a compliment, look the person directly in their eyes and say, "Thank you." No deflection allowed. It will be awkward at first, but keep at it; it will be worth it. I promise.

When you win a raffle (even if the prize is only a pen), celebrate—thank the organizer, then scream, do the funky chicken, and tell all of your friends. Or you could simply smile; the point is just do not complain. Complaining is not allowed in Luckieville.

Making an effort to accept the good that comes your way will not only make you a more likeable person, but it will also increase your self-confidence—both traits of Luckies.

Let's Leave You with an Affirmation

"I am worthy of all good that comes my way."

CODE B

BLAME GAME— CHOOSE TO SIT OUT!

If there is one game that Luckies sit out, it's the Blame Game. They know that no one comes out of this game a winner, ever, and they understand that blaming another individual for their blunder shows more about their own character than that of the person being blamed.

Individuals having a tough time getting lucky in life (let's call them "Unluckies") are usually the star players of the blame game. They're blaming coworkers for something going south in the office, an ex for their current insecurities, parents for not being there, and the list goes on. It is *always* someone else's fault. If this sounds familiar, it's time to throw in the towel and sit out the game permanently. The more time we spend focusing on who is to blame, the less time we have to find a solution and move on.

This is not to say that others don't mistakes, or that another's actions cannot impact us gravely; rather, the point is that highlighting another's downfall does not do us any good. Reflecting shade only doubles it. Sidestep it altogether and move into the light. Luckies gleam with positivity, and you shall too.

Oftentimes, fault is a two-way street, and you may use blame to showcase the other culprit in an attempt to reduce your own liability. Luckies, however, realize that everyone around them is an image of themselves in some way, and in every situation there is a lesson to be learned. They own their role in the situation, they apologize if they had a hand in the error, and they move on.

How to Apply Code B:
Blame Game—Choose to Sit Out in Daily Life

When the next incident occurs where you have a tendency to play the blame game, take a deep breath. Then ask yourself the following questions:

Did I play a role in this occurrence?

Even if you were only the observer, that's a role. Own it.

What can I do right this moment to defuse the problem?

By busying the mind with a call for action, the impulse to blame is shoved aside.

What is the lesson in this situation?

Every incident has a lesson. Ponder it until you find yours.

Quote-Worthy

"How few there are who have courage enough to own their faults, or resolution enough to mend them."

– Benjamin Franklin

— · — ·

CODE C

CHARACTER BUILDING

As the new year rolls in, gyms swiftly fill up with individuals wanting to get their bodies in better shape for the upcoming summer. Many people also have financial, vocational, and even educational goals as priorities. But how many of us actually set goals to develop our character? To be more charismatic? Better listeners? More understanding? More tolerant? To hold better conversations? To be an all-around better version of ourselves compared to years past?

Luckies put a solid amount of time and effort into improving their character. They converse with and observe others with qualities that they admire and make mental notes. They watch TED Talks, attend seminars, and read self-help books. They discuss their challenges with mentors and life coaches. So what is it that Luckies understand that others don't? They recognize the true value of character building. They realize that their likability puts them in the right places at the right time, with the "who's who" in life. Improving their character allows them to brand themselves in a way others cannot. Their character-building endeavors—their self-branding, in a sense—pays them lifelong dividends.

Folks who are successful in life hang around other successful people, and not for the reasons you may think. It isn't because they think they are better than everyone else; it is because like attracts like. They seek others who uplift their spirits and inspire them to be more intelligent. To be wealthier. To give more of themselves. Oprah Winfrey, who I think we can all agree is a Luckie, once said, "Surround yourself with only people who are going to take you higher." Oprah clearly understands the power of character building.

Our character, the traits that make us who we are, has many layers. This makes building a better character an ongoing process, and we don't want to hamper our progress with the likes of envy and jealousy. When you use Code C, you are not intimidated by the successes of others, but instead celebrate with them and probe them for tips, with the confidence that you too will soon get there. Downplaying other people's success by highlighting their pitfalls, or simply disliking them for what they have, is a surefire way to remain down and out. We do not have to like everyone that crosses our path, but we should respect them and their life journey. This entails holding our tongue if we have nothing pleasant to say. There is an Arab proverb that goes, "The words of the tongue should have three gate keepers: Is it true? Is it kind? Is it necessary?" We can all benefit from considering these gate keepers every time we are tempted to speak ill of another.

How to Apply Code C:
Character Building in Daily Life

There are so many things that we can do to better our character. Being a Luckie is truly all about the choices we make. Let's take a look at a few that will be easy for you to begin with:

- Respect all walks of life. Treat the street sweeper with the same respect as the Fortune 500 CEO, regardless of who is watching.

- Offer your knowledge to others without expecting anything in return.

- Understand that everyone, regardless of background, race, faith, or gender, has something to offer.

- Every year, set a New Year's resolution that benefits your character, and let this be the one resolution you actually keep.

- Watch TED Talks (on TED.com, YouTube, or even Netflix), attend character-building seminars (there's an amazing variety and quantity of options out there), and read more self-improvement books (thanks for choosing this one!). Check out the Resources section of this book for more suggestions.

Quote Me on This One Because It Bears Repeating

"Your character-building endeavors, your self-branding, will pay you lifelong dividends."

– Gayneté Edwards

CODE D

DRESS FOR SUCCESS

A few years back, when I was a management trainee at a local bank, a senior vice president introduced me to a quote that I now keep near and dear to my heart, "Dress for the job you want, not for the one you have." I was already wearing tailored suits quite regularly and always ensured that I was well groomed; the adage "First impressions are lasting impressions" often echoed in the back of my mind. This new quote, however, more accurately described why I dressed the way I did; I just hadn't been able to put it into words until then. At the end of my program, the senior vice president, along with the vice president in the department, wanted me to join their team. In the end, I decided to go to another area, but I know that had I worked just as hard, yet looked a righteous mess, the proposal would not have been made.

Whether you're aspiring to be a top manager, a nurse, a poet, a hairstylist, a painter, or a rock star, the premise remains the same. Always make sure that you are presenting your very best side to the public, because you never know if your future boss/client/fan is watching. We do not verbally communicate with everyone that we see on a daily basis (can you imagine how tiring that would be?), so our outward appearance speaks volumes in those moments when we cannot. Let's face it; we live in a society where everything is instantaneous, including someone's impression of you before formally meeting you. Luckies understand this notion quite well and, as a result, present themselves to the public (including on social media!) in a way that supports their heart's desire. Take a brief moment to think about what message you are sending to the world. Are your aspirations reflected in the way you present yourself?

I am not saying that expensive suits are required to be a Luckie. But a clean appearance—shoes in good condition, clothing that fits well, and a groomed head (and nails!)—will get you noticed by the right people for all of the right reasons, regardless of your desires in life. Instead of using that extra five minutes in the morning to check the latest Facebook and Instagram posts, polish/wipe off your shoes, brush your hair, and spray on a fragrance (less is always more). If we do not show that we value our appearance, we will be devalued by society. Cold. Hard. Truth.

How to Apply Code D:
Dress for Success in Daily Life

It's the simple things that we often overlook, like an iron. (Use one.) I can only imagine my mom toppling over with laughter at this one; an iron is my arch nemesis, but nonetheless, I do value and appreciate its importance in polishing my overall appearance. Smile on, Mom.

If you need more appropriate clothing for your journey to Luckieville, but you are financially down and out (but not for long, you future Luckie!), there are many options available, such as clothing barns, discount stores, and yard sales. Or you can learn how to sew (see Code H: Hobby—Get a Good One!).

Everything else comes down to hygiene and observing how the Luckies around you present themselves. You see, us Luckies and soon-to-be-Luckies make no excuses on our journey to Luckieville. We show up ready to chase our dreams, ensuring we dress the part—and we succeed as a result.

A Quote Worth Remembering

"If you put a small value upon yourself, rest assured that the world will not raise your price."

– Unknown

CODE E

ELIMINATE THE NEGATIVITY

This code could easily fill up the rest of this book; it's that important to Luckies. Negativity is a dark, powerful energy. Negativity will win every time, if you allow it, but with practice you can identify and eliminate negativity the way Luckies do. We will look at eliminating negativity in three different areas of life: Self, Others, and Surrounding Environment—what I like to call "S.O.S." This is an apt term because if all three of these areas are drowning in negativity, you'll be in desperate need of help and Luckieville will be a mere fantasy—until the elimination process begins, that is. I may come across a little harshly on this one, but in order to join the Luckies, it must sink in. Luckies avoid negativity like the plague, and so shall you.

Self

Self, the most important of the three areas, is first on our list. Do you find that there is *always* something that goes wrong? When birthdays and holidays roll around, do you wonder what all the fuss is about and prefer not to join the festivities? Is it *always* raining the day that you clean your car? Does your boss *always* pick on you? Do you hate Mondays, and all weekdays for that matter? Do you dub payday "pay-out day," because the money is here today, gone tomorrow? If you answered yes to more than one of these questions, chances are you are a pessimistic individual who finds the undesirable in every situation. But let me guess: you're not a pessimist, you're a realist, right?

Well here's a dose of "real" for you: you have created your reality. And until you eliminate the negativity, your reality will remain the same. Think about this one for a moment. I'll wait.

You must be accountable for your words, actions, and projections into this world. If they are always negative, they have a negative impact on others, not to mention the damage to you as an individual. What role are you playing in these horrible circumstances? Are things really terrible, *all* the time? Begin noticing when you wash the car and the sun shines the whole time. And if it does, in fact, rain every single time, begin using a little more common sense and check the weather first.

Notice when your boss is sitting at her desk, engrossed in work instead of picking on you. Notice and embrace the moment. Also question whether her "complaints" are actually well-intentioned and valid. Are you truly doing the best that you can with what you have? The liability may very well be yours. (Note that it is also highly probable that your superior is a negative person herself, and we will look at how to deal with that shortly.)

Now for the king of all negativity: complaints about money. Complaining about your lack of funds never makes your financial situation any better, and it drains the energy of those around you that have to listen. Stop complaining immediately, then make an honest attempt to rectify the problem. If you constantly whine that payday is pay-out day, you may very well be living above your means. Do you buy lunch more than twice a week or buy a coffee daily? Or even buy alcohol on a weekly basis? Keep all of your receipts and add them up at month's end. You will likely note that your money is not being used as wisely as it could be. Is your electricity bill killing you? Research innovative ways to cut it down; the solution could be as simple as unplugging something overnight. Luckies are very conscious of their spending habits. Understand yours and find ways to slash unnecessary expenses.

If you already budget wisely and have reduced spending where you can, and you are really not making enough money, there are always options. If you are a hard worker, make a proposal for an increase and discuss it with your boss (or put some serious effort into obtaining a new job that pays more). You can also consider starting an at-home/online business for extra income if you have a special skill that you have mastered. If you don't have any skills you've mastered, read Code H: Hobby—Get a Good One. We must find a way, not an excuse. Being Luckie is not always easy; if it were, everyone would do it. It is very attainable, though, if we muster up the courage to work hard towards our goals using these codes. No negativity is allowed in Luckieville, especially when it relates to money.

None of the above sounding familiar yet? Great! Before we leave the topic of self, however, we must discuss negative self-talk. Do you beat yourself up inside and think that you are not good enough for something or someone? Do you always think that the words coming out of your mouth sound stupid? Do you try to dress for success but nothing looks right on your body? Self-doubt is an ugly monster. Try affirmations to assist you in developing self-love (there are thousands merely a Google search away!). You must realize that you are worthy of good. Until this occurs, good will hide just around the corner.

Others

Do you find yourself surrounded by people who are constantly nagging and complaining? Remove yourself. Fast. These people are the equivalent of secondhand smoke. Although the negativity is not coming from you, it is equally as toxic. If you cannot readily get away from Nagging Nancy and Blaming Bill at work, try plugging in headphones or changing the subject to eliminate the negativity. If the culprit is a family member that you live with, try going for regular walks to clear your head.

Having a mature conversation with the perpetrator to explain how their behavior affects you may also prove beneficial. They may not be aware that they are so negative and will be thankful for the frank feedback. Not quite the type for confrontation? Try an email or a letter. Even if you do not send it, it will help you clarify your feelings towards the situation until you build up the courage or an alternate plan of attack. You can even try recommending this book. Whatever you do, do not participate. Where your active responsiveness shows, negativity grows. Ignore them. If you find that none of the solutions above work, begin looking for another job/place to live. When all else fails, Luckies learn to love negative individuals from a distance. We cannot control others. We can, however, control our own actions and how we interact with others.

Surrounding Environment

Is your home, place of employment, or another place where you spend a lot of time overwhelmingly grimy, damaged beyond repair, overly cluttered due to hoarding, or the popular loitering area where questionable activity takes place? It's time to change this—quickly. Oftentimes we overlook the importance of our surrounding environment and how it affects our well-being. Luckily, the solutions to improve your surrounding environment are no-brainers—fix it or move. No excuses; every problem has a solution. If you are the reason for the dirty environment, commit to changing your ways. No one is perfect; accept your faults and get professional help. We cannot expect to welcome positive results in an unwelcoming atmosphere. The two just do not mix.

Many Luckies have professional help around the house, and not because they cannot find anything better to spend their money on or cannot do it for themselves. Luckies realize the importance of a clean environment and know that the time that they would normally spend doing housework, can be spent on something in alignment with their Luckie goals (see Codes C, H, N, and S for some examples). You do not have to rush to hire a cleaner right now; just realize the importance of a clean environment and remember that there is always a trade-off.

How to Apply Code E:
Eliminate the Negativity in Daily Life

I've already provided ample solutions to assist with the elimination of negativity in your life, so this recap will be fairly short. If you truly want to become a Luckie, avoid negative words, self-talk, people, and environments at all costs. Music can be a great support as you make the necessary changes. Not only do headphones help to block out the negative chaos, but listening to music that you enjoy has a way of taking you to another place in time, changing your mood almost immediately.

It is important to remember that we are not perfect and negative thoughts, feelings, and words are bound to creep in from time to time, even more so when we are just starting out on our journey to Luckieville. The key is to not to beat yourself up about it, and don't let the negative crowd out the positive.

Some Great Quotables

"If you have good thoughts, they will shine out of your face like sun beams and you will always look lovely."
– Ronald Dahl

"A negative attitude is like a flat tire. You can't go anywhere until you change it."
– Unknown

"People inspire you or they drain you—pick them wisely."
– Hans F. Hanson

"You are a product of your environment. So choose the environment that will best develop you toward your objective. Analyze your life in terms of its environment. Are the things around you

helping you toward success—or are they holding you back?"

– W. Clement Stone

CODE F

FREE YOURSELF FROM MIND CLUTTER

Clutter in any form is restrictive. Clutter—in the house, at work, and especially in the mind—slows us down tremendously. The latest lesson I have learned on my road to Luckieville is the benefit of a clutter-free mind. A cluttered mind can prevent us from seeing key opportunities that would have been obvious had we not been focused on something else that didn't require our immediate attention. Golden opportunities (also known as "lucky coincidences that never happen to me" by the Unluckies) are snatched up quickly by the Luckies.

With millions of to-dos running through our heads at the office and at home, it is easy to create a mental Mount Everest of tasks. However, it is impossible to work on everything at one time, so it's best to focus only on what you should be working on at that very moment. The more demands placed on you, the more you need to take an extra few minutes to write out a to-do list. Getting everything out of your head, then prioritizing that list and working on tasks in order of priority, can reduce mental clutter so you can perform at your best. Even if you do not get to everything on your list, you will have a clear picture of what needs to be done next, eliminating the stress of worrying that you'll forget what needs to be done.

Focusing on to-dos beyond the present moment is distracting and can decrease your production and accuracy—not an option for thriving individuals. Being as efficient as possible is a key quality shared by Luckies, and the reasons are clear as the summer sky: time is too precious a commodity to waste, and great productivity gets you noticed by employers and clients alike, immediately pushing you ahead of the average, minimum-effort Unluckie. So get to decluttering that brain!

How to Apply Code F:
Free Yourself from Mind Clutter in Daily Life

Make a to-do list for the day/week/month, whichever works best for you. You can also make a digital list, or get an app. Remember, no excuses! Begin checking off the items as you complete them and do not beat yourself up about what could not be done. Set realistic daily, weekly, and monthly goals. You will feel great as you begin noticing that your time does not fly by wasted, but is used productively.

Next, you mustn't put off phone calls and emails. Do you have a friend that you've been meaning to catch up with? Add him or her to the to-do list and get to it. These items never really leave the mind unless fulfilled, and the back of your mind is probably screaming for a release.

Have a sick loved one or another stressful situation on your mind? Make dealing with this a priority. Not something that can be easily dealt with? Talk it over with someone willing to listen. Sometimes a listening ear is the best remedy for stress and mind clutter.

Feeling overwhelmed? Make a checklist of what is important to you and cut out what isn't. The great thing about being an adult is that we can choose what we wish to do. Never feel pressured to partake in activities, events, and unnecessary gatherings—cut the clutter!

Code S: Surround Yourself in Solitude can also help you reduce mind clutter.

Let's Leave You with a Passage, Shall We?

"Never again clutter your days or nights with so many menial

and unimportant things that you have no time to accept a real challenge when it comes along. This applies to play as well as work. A day merely survived is no cause for celebration. You are not here to fritter away your precious hours when you have the ability to accomplish so much by making a slight change in your routine. No more busy work. No more hiding from success. Leave time, leave space, to grow. Now. Now! Not tomorrow!"

– Og Mandino

— — .

CODE G

GIVE GRACIOUSLY

There is much to say about a philanthropic heart. To give of our time, labor, and/or money to better the position of another in need is truly a beautiful thing. To give it kindly, without expectations of receiving anything in return, is even better. Regardless of whether you believe in the principal of causality—the idea that what you do now (positive or negative) comes back to you at a future date—giving back should always be a no-brainer if you want to be a Luckie.

Assisting others keeps our own lives in perspective. We realize just how fortunate we already are, opening the doorway for more blessings to arrive. To be able to provide aid to those in need also makes us feel good about ourselves. This self-confidence from feeling like an essential piece of this world's puzzle gives life new meaning. We have a chance to make a real difference and become heroes without a cape, and who doesn't want to be a hero?

Luckies always give back where they can, whether through financial donations, mentoring, or simply being the middleman (or middlewoman) connecting someone in need with the person who can help. Because Luckies are so involved with communities and aware of the communities' needs, they have more opportunities for networking. This allows Luckies to not only spend time around like-minded, positive individuals, but also increases their public profile. They get opportunities for photo ops and press releases, which makes them even more visible. Visibility, especially for charity efforts, often increases likeability. Note—public profile boosts can merely be one of the many benefits of giving graciously and should not, I repeat, *should not*, be the reason for wanting to give. Give graciously of your time, energy, and money to worthy causes and expect nothing in return. You will then find that you get everything in return in ways you never expected. Though the rewards of giving are often instantaneous, our sole focus should be to assist those in need.

If doing physical labor, remain upbeat and be considerate of everyone involved, in an attempt to lift the spirits of those you are assisting. If donating financially, research the best fit for your dollar. What are you passionate about? Once you figure this out and make a donation, follow the money, being sure to find out exactly how it will be used and following up to see if it has been done. Even if only donating a minimal amount, don't be afraid to ask the question. It is your hard-earned dollar and you deserve to know that it will not be squandered.

How to Apply Code G:
Give Graciously in Daily Life

If new to giving, start by determining what's most important to you. Is it relationships? Then you may find joy in assisting families in need or abused individuals, reading to children, or even donating to shelters. If it is a safer environment you care about—for your own and future generations—help reduce violence and violent acts by applying to be a reserve police officer, or by donating funds to local charities to combat drugs and poverty through community education initiatives. Does a healthier environment have your heart? Start this one at home by recycling, using reusable containers, and reducing consumption. If a healthy body is important to you, support efforts to find cures for diseases near and dear to your heart or even start a walking club to assist with the prevention of heart disease. Is educating future generations important to you? Offer to volunteer at local schools, mentor a child, start an etiquette camp, or create a reading club. Get involved and get your loved ones involved as well. The options are truly boundless.

If the suggestions above seem like a bit too much to take on at the moment, start smaller and closer to the home. Offer to watch the child of a relative who needs a break for a few hours or go over and read to them. Gestures from the heart are always appreciated. Spend time with an older relative: teach them how to use a computer, or ask them to teach you to knit or explain their history. When interacting, actually take the time out to listen to what the person is saying and provide sound advice/feedback. Giving graciously of ourselves, by donating money, time, and efforts, is easy and can be lots of fun.

Quote-Worthy Ladies and Gents Who Know about Giving Back

"A life not lived for others is not a life."

– Mother Teresa

"No one has ever become poor from giving."

– Anne Frank

"We make a living by what we get, but we make a life by what we give."

– Winston Churchill

"At the end of the day, it's not about what you have or even what you've accomplished... it's about who you've lifted up, who you've made better. It's about what you've given back."

– Denzel Washington

CODE H

HOBBY—GET A GOOD ONE!

Collins English Dictionary defines the word *hobby* as "an activity pursued in spare time for pleasure or relaxation." By this definition I believe it is safe to say that we all have hobbies, though some may be more productive than others. The difference between the hobbies of Luckies and those of Unluckies is that Luckies have hobbies that increase their successes in life.

What we do in our leisure time is equally as important as what we do in our most productive hours. Essentially, every hour spent awake should be used in such a way that we find ourselves growing daily. This does not mean that we cannot relax; rather, it's how we relax that makes all the difference. Watching hours of reality drama mind filth versus watching television that feeds the brain (or lifts our spirits). Playing video games for hours versus spending quality time with our children. Spending quiet moments thinking about all the bad that has happened versus spending a moment meditating (see Code S: Surround Yourself in Solitude). And by far the most important when it comes to hobbies: learning a new skill to be "good enough" versus learning that same skill to be the best we can be at it.

Remember the figure of speech "Jack of all trades, master of none"? Let's not be that person. Skills are meant to be mastered, not just learned, and this mastery can greatly assist you on the road to Luckieville. Take care when selecting a skill to develop, because it will take time to perfect it. I do not want any excuses on this one. We all have spare time—even if just one hour a week. Mark Cuban and Tyler Perry have the same 24 hours as we do, and they have no doubt chosen to perfect their crafts.

Whether your hobby is website building, carpentry, quilting, sewing, script writing, reading, cooking, golf, or investments—become an expert! Being an expert makes your skills sellable. Yes, even reading and golf! Avid readers tend to be great writers. Readers can write a blog and get paid advertisers on it, start a reading club, write reviews for a local paper, or find a gap in the market and write a book—getting the picture yet? Aside from improving your overall health and providing ample networking opportunities, if you become an expert at golf, you can begin teaching others or even host your own tournaments. Who knows: perhaps with the money earned, you can purchase land and create your own golf course. With enough effort, you can be in a PGA tournament.

Do not place limits on where you can go with your skills. Ever. The key is to realize that you have limitless opportunities if you market yourself and your mastered skills well enough, and having limitless opportunities is what being a Luckie is all about.

So how does one master a skill? Practice, train, learn from the work of other masters, and repeat. If you pass your time watching Bloomberg and find a true interest in investments, begin reading books on the subject or take a course. Go even further and get a professional designation. Yes, mastering a skill can be hard work (see Code R: Roll Up Your Sleeves), but working hard on something you enjoy, your true passion, is also lots of fun!

Even if you are happy with your current streams of income and do not wish to pursue a hobby for that purpose, mastering it is still a good idea. When you become great at something (or make up your mind to become great), you will find many people popping out of the woodwork that are interested in the same thing, much like when you want to buy a new car you begin noticing others with the same model that you have had your eyes on. It's funny how the universe works to support us through this kind of synchronicity. You can meet people almost anywhere—on the golf course, at a knitting club or reading club, on the basketball court, in an investment course, etc.—that will assist you with mastering your skill. These people will be from all walks of life, can provide many valuable lessons, and will help you to broaden your network.

If you'd like to spend all of your spare time building a stronger relationship with your family, this too is perfectly acceptable and shares the same rewards and then some. Attend the latest family events in the community, read books to help you understand teenagers a bit better, cook with them, play golf with them, draw *with* them—master a skill with them! Why not turn the whole family into Luckies?

How to Apply Code H:
Hobby—Get a Good One in Daily Life

Sit down and take a moment to figure out what you would be interested in pursuing in the spare time that you have. Then set out to do it. It's really that simple. It comes down to making up your mind that you want to grow and finding a hobby that assists you in this endeavor.

Once you figure out which hobby to pursue, talk to people who already do it and find out how they got started. Read the local newspaper to find out what community events are happening, or do an online search to find out what's available in your area. If there's a sport you want to take up, go to where it is normally played and ask questions. If your passions are more along the lines of cooking or jewelry making, go to a cooking supply store or jeweler to find out how to get started. Once you know how to begin, the next step is to figure out what timing works best for your schedule, then commit to begin.

If you already have a hobby that you pursue, good for you! You are one step closer to Luckieville. Ensure that you are putting your all into mastering your hobby. Read all that you can about the subject. Interact with others who do the same thing. Never settle for being "good enough" and always do your absolute best. You will notice that as your skills begin to improve, so will your confidence, network, and passion for it. At the very least, you will find that you are very happy with yourself, and what's greater than happiness?

Let's Leave You with a Quote on This One

"Happy is the man who can make a living by his hobby."
– George Bernard Shaw

CODE I

INDEBTEDNESS— JUST A FANCY WORD FOR GRATITUDE

Oftentimes we are so busy living in the future of want and desire that we forget to live in the moment, in the now, and count our blessings that have already arrived. Luckies understand the importance of showing their appreciation for the great things that happen on a daily basis, and so shall you. Life's blessings are too awesome to ignore!

You may not yet have that great-looking car that you want, but you do have the gas money to fill up the car you have right now. Smile with that thought. You may not have won the latest raffle prize, but you did have the money to donate to the cause. That in itself is worth celebrating. Perhaps you go to a store to purchase something that you have had your eye on and discover it is on sale—bonus! Just noticing the small "lucky breaks" that come your way daily goes a long way in increasing them. Feeling gratitude, or indebtedness, makes us warm and fuzzy inside, and when we are happy, we cannot be negative—are you seeing the correlation yet? Brian Tracy (speaker, best-selling author, entrepreneur, and success expert) once said, "Develop an attitude of gratitude, and give thanks for everything that happens to you, knowing that every step forward is a step toward achieving something bigger and better than your current situation."

Great things happen every day. We wake up to a loving family and great friends. We find the perfect parking spot, we are let out of a busy intersection by a kind individual, and we receive warm smiles from complete strangers all the time. It is our job to notice these things, appreciate them, and say, "Thank you." Unluckies tend to get the idea of gratitude backwards. They feel that Luckies have no choice but to be grateful because they have everything to be grateful for. But Luckies are aware that "luck" comes through understanding and practicing the codes in this book, in particular by noticing and appreciating what they have already. In other words, "luck" follows gratitude, not the other way around.

How to Apply Code I:
Indebtedness—Just a Fancy Word for Gratitude in Daily Life

Before you go to sleep, take a moment to think about all of the great things that have happened throughout the day. What are you grateful for? Luckies do not wait until Thanksgiving to appreciate these things. Let this be your last thought before dozing off and you'll wake in a great mood.

Many Luckies (including me) write their daily "lucky breaks" in a gratitude journal. You may find this helpful for you too. The journal doesn't have to be fancy; just a book with blank pages will do. Make an effort to write daily and date each entry.

Practice using positive gratitude affirmations in the morning, like the ones below!

Indebtedness (Gratitude) Affirmations

"Life is so awesome. I have so much to be thankful for each day!"

"This day will be filled with many moments of happiness. Thank you!"

"So many blessings come my way. I am so thankful for seeing another day!"

"The abundance of love in my life is evident. I am soooo lucky!"

"Prosperity follows me around every corner of my life. I am so grateful!"

. — — —

CODE J

JOKE IS ON YOU

Remember that you are capable of anything that you set your mind to. Work your very hardest to achieve it, but if you don't get what you wished and worked so hard for, realize that it is because it is not meant for you at this moment. It may help to think of life as a game of tug-of-war between our own visions of what is meant for us to do/have versus our divine plan—the one that is best and meant for us. When we fall on our behinds in this tug-of-war game of life, we must laugh at ourselves for fighting against the grain! Whether we call the creator of this divine plan God, the universe, our higher self, all of the above, something else, or don't believe in a higher power at all, the basis remains the same—when our plan does not work, we must expect something much greater to come to us instead. With this expectation, we cannot help but win.

The ultimate "luck" in life is to be happy. The quickest way to get there is to not take life so seriously and to laugh at our stumbles along the way. I am not saying that a hearty belly laugh is needed to be happy—wait, yes I am. Laugh. Often. Take a look at the children around you and how happy the smallest things make them. Their laughter echoes in the hearts of loved ones, spreading infectious joy to everyone around them. We were once those children, but somehow we have allowed bills and a 9–5 to consume that cheerfulness. This should not be the case. In fact, a serious demeanor doesn't improve or reduce the stresses of life but amplifies them instead. It takes more muscles to frown than to smile, and that fact alone should encourage us to crack one every so often—it's less work on our part!

Smile and appreciate that you qualified for that loan. Laugh at your naive younger self who couldn't wait to grow up and get a "real job." Welcome to adulthood, a theme park created by our past thoughts and actions. Now if you make your current ones a bit more jolly, you can make your future a bit brighter.

Take a morbid walk with me for just a moment. If you died at this very moment, would you be happy with what you have accomplished? Material belongings aside, are you happy with the hearts you have touched, and the lessons you have taught and learned along the way? With the time you have spent with loved ones, with the legacy you have left behind—are you satisfied? If so, great! If not, chances are you are taking life a little too seriously. At the end of the day, when the curtains close and a body is put six feet under, no one is going to say "Man, I loved how seriously she took life." They will, however, remember the person's smile, her laughter, her positive outlook on life. These are the things that we should really want to pass on to our children. They are the only riches that truly matter in the end. If you thought success, money, and expensive possessions was all a "lucky" life was about, the joke is on you! Laugh it off, super star.

How to Apply Code J:
Joke Is on You in Daily Life

To become a Luckie, I am not suggesting that you walk around with a huge smile that doesn't erase or that you laugh nonstop. That would be insanity. I am not even suggesting that you have to be happy every moment of every day. That isn't realistic; you are human and will be down in the dumps on occasion. You do, however, need to ensure that your happy moments easily outweigh the ones spent sulking, and I have a few suggestions to help you to get there:

- Spend more time around children. Their innocence and contentment with life is contagious. Soak it up!

- Make a conscious effort to smile and laugh more often. Smile at strangers; they may really be in need of a sincere smile.

- Give back. You will find that helping others helps you to realize just how much you have to be thankful for. If that isn't a reason to smile, I don't know what is.

- Watch and read things that make you laugh out loud. For me, the show to watch when I want a good laugh is The Big Bang Theory—I find the show's main character, Sheldon Cooper, terrifyingly hilarious.

- Do not hold grudges. Keeping anger inside of you is the equivalent of drinking a toxic elixir. The longer you hold on to it, the more you drink and the deadlier it becomes. Anger kills joy so quickly. For this reason, I have personally made a vow not to hold grudges. I refuse to give my energy to a situation that upsets me for too long. I play it through my mind, accept it for what it is, and mentally wish the infuriating person or situation the best and make the conscious choice to focus my thoughts on something more positive.

Keep things in perspective. At any given moment there will be someone, somewhere, going through something similar or tougher. Remembering this can help us keep life's not-so-great moments in perspective. At the same time, avoid becoming the victim of others' problems; refer to Code E: Eliminate the Negativity (the Others section) and Code K: Know When to Let Go if this is what is stopping you from being happy.

Achieving happiness is often easier said than done, especially if facing a serious issue such as depression or bipolar disorder. If this is true to your case, please seek help. Reach out to family and friends and professionals in the field.

Quote Me on This One

"The ultimate 'luck' in life is to be happy. The quickest way to get there is to not take life so seriously and to laugh at our stumbles along the way."

– Gayneté Edwards

CODE K

KNOW WHEN TO LET GO

Is there anyone in your life who makes you cringe when you hear their name? Who brings you down the second you hear their voice? Who drains your energy? Is there anyone in your life who abuses you? If so, it's time to consider letting them go. Not everyone that comes into our lives is meant to stay. Some come to teach lifelong lessons of love. Others come to teach shorter lessons of humility, patience, and fortitude. It is up to us to know when a person's time in our lives has expired. As stated in Code E: Eliminate the Negativity, Luckies identify those who hinder their growth and happiness and learn to love them from a distance. They do not lose their love for those people, but understand that if they continue interacting with them, they will begin to lose parts of themselves. Code K goes beyond just a negative individual, however, into the realm of excessive neediness, using, and abusing.

We tend to give so much of ourselves and our resources to loved ones with the intention to help, but sometimes, unconsciously, we create a codependency. Some people do not wish to change their circumstances, as much as they tell us that they do. Start paying close attention to their actions versus their words. Someone deserving of our love, time, and efforts would make a genuine attempt to improve their circumstances and will not make us feel as if it is an obligation of ours to serve them. Countless individuals are simply empty and angry with life; no matter what we do, we cannot fill that void. It has to be fixed on their end. Step away and love them from a distance.

Don't get me wrong—many people in our lives may genuinely need our help to get back on their feet financially, to get over a break up, or to work through another difficult situation. In this case, it is temporary and we should give without expecting anything in return. There is nothing wrong with financially assisting a person who needs a little help if you are able to do so or offering kind words of encouragement to a friend or family member in need. It is when a person's ills become your own or a person begins attacking you that a problem arises. When their troubles start taking a toll on your happiness, you must step back and decide just how much more you can give without losing yourself in the process. It is a hard choice to walk out of someone's life, especially when you feel that you are all that person has, but you won't be any help if you too are broken as a result of the interaction or relationship. Love yourself enough to know when to step away from a loved one who is hurting you.

Our relationships play such a crucial role in our ability to be Luckies. Creating a winning team around us is a surefire way to "win." The opposite is also true. If surrounded by negativity and misuse/abuse, we will "lose." Teach your loved ones the lessons that you have learned in this book—those tools may go a lot further than money ever could in improving their circumstances.

How to Apply Code K:
Know When to Let Go in Daily Life

Much of knowing when to let go comes down to taking a step back and asking yourself the following questions: 1) Am I being used and/or abused? 2) Am I truly helping this person by remaining in his or her life? 3) Is this person hindering me and my growth? It is not selfish to worry about other people's impact on your life. If you don't, who will? If you feel that the problems are beyond you, recommend professional help. Use your newfound Luckie connections to direct them to charities, groups, financial assistance, or someone else you feel will do a better job helping them. If they're in genuine need, they will thank you.

When you receive a call from an adult in your life who falls into any of the above categories, watch to see if they even bother to ask about you and your day, or go straight into pouring their problems on to you. If they never do ask, chances are they are too self-absorbed to realize that your life matters too. If they do not care, why do you? Realize that just like you, they too are responsible for the choices that they make. Be strong. If you make up your mind to step away, do so.

Affirmations to Assist

"I attract great relationships in my life and am worthy of the love received."

"I give what I can and let go of what I cannot, knowing that all will be well."

"I am wise enough to know when I have had enough and strong enough to let go."

• — • •

CODE L

LISTEN TO YOUR HEART

We all have it—that natural instinct that tells us when something is right (and equally as important, when it isn't). Some call it a gut feeling, a feeling in the pit of the stomach that gives them all the information that they need to know. For me, I get a heavy feeling in my chest that serves as a warning, and a warming passion in the chest when I need to pursue something. Others cannot explain exactly what it is that they get other than they "just know." This feeling tells us whether or not to do something, say something, or go somewhere. You may not feel it every time you have a serious decision to make, but when you do, you need to go with it. Always.

Luckies pay attention to the signs, listen to their bodies, and, most importantly, act on those gut feelings. Writing a book was always in the back of my mind, but when the thought began to be accompanied by that warm feeling in my chest, I knew I had to stop just thinking about it and begin writing. If only one person is positively impacted, this book has served its purpose. We all have goals and dreams—many that would fall by the wayside if we allowed our mind to make all of the decisions for us. This is because in its logical innocence, it is fearful by nature, scared of failing. Our heart knows better; it knows that we can accomplish absolutely anything if only we can trick our mind into following us on the journey and our butts into working themselves into a frenzy to ensure our success.

Many greats, from Patti LaBelle to Steve Jobs, have spoken about the importance of following our heart and our passions. Passion is a desire felt deep within our soul, something that cannot be found on an x-ray, but can be seen on canvases, in music lyrics, in the pages of a great book, on stages worldwide, on the basketball court, and the list goes on. It is clear that Luckies follow their hearts all the time. This code does not mean that we are to abandon reason by any means; it is simply calling us to follow our passions, without letting the fear of failure stop us from pursing that which we are meant to do. We must not be impulsive, but must follow our pulse, our drive, our passions, our heart.

How to Apply Code L:
Listen to Your Heart in Daily Life

Many great things come to us in our silence. Our heart's true desires are no different. Refer to Code S: Surround Yourself in Solitude to see how a moment of silence can help you listen to your heart.

Grab a piece of paper (right now!) and write down what it is that you would enjoy doing and would want to accomplish if you were free of fear and had all the necessary resources available.

Once you are clear on what you want, create a vision board! If you haven't created one before, go on YouTube or Google to find step-by-step guidance. Look at your vision board every day and feel yourself accomplishing all that you have on it. Take small action steps daily to get you that much closer to your dreams.

Surround yourself with passionate individuals; their passion will begin to rub off on you. Get a mentor (see Code M: Mentors Are a Power Source) and consider getting a life coach; he or she can assist you with finding and following your inner voice.

If we can justify working hard for someone else 9–5 every weekday, we must find no excuse to stop us from working hard towards our own dreams and desires. Tony Gaskins said, "If you don't build your own dream, someone else will hire you to build theirs."

My Absolute Favorite "Listen to Your Heart" Quote

"Your time is limited, so don't waste it living someone else's life. Don't be trapped by dogma—which is living with the results of other people's thinking. Don't let the noise of others' opinions

drown out your own inner voice. And most important, have the courage to follow your heart and intuition. They somehow already know what you truly want to become. Everything else is secondary."

– Steve Jobs

CODE M

MENTORS ARE A POWER SOURCE

Mentors are more important than most folk realize; they are the power source for success. This is because much like a car needs gas to run, Luckies too need a form of gas, and it's one that mentors provide so well. G.A.S. in this instance stands for Guidance, Accountability, and Support. These three combine for a winning combination on the road to Luckieville. I have two mentors and they are amazing; their G.A.S. has been instrumental in helping me get where I want to go.

Before we continue, it should be clarified that mentors can make awesome role models, but not all role models are great mentors. A mentor is a Luckie individual with experience and expertise in a certain field (or fields) who invests his or her time and efforts in grooming a less-experienced individual to develop personally and/or professionally. Therefore, mentors are not just people we can look up to, but experts who assist us in becoming someone that others can look up to as well. This does not mean that the mentor must always be older or wiser than the mentee (though this is usually the case); they just have experience where the mentee does not. You may find that your mentors have mentors of their own; Luckies understand that there is always room for development.

Guidance

Although we sometimes like to think that we know all of the answers, it cannot be further from the truth. Aside from answering our many questions and providing sound advice relating to our careers, education, and life goals in general, based on their invaluable experience, mentors also tend to have many useful contacts to help us to grow our networks and self-brands. For instance, through my first mentor, I was introduced to my second mentor, a finance coach, as well as other movers and shakers in my community. As our own networks grow, we have access to more people whom we can bounce ideas off of, who may know about job opportunities, and who may even become future mentors.

Accountability

Communication is a key element in any mentor-mentee relationship. Mentors are in constant contact with their mentees and usually want to know what they are currently doing to grow in their career/business so they know how to push them to advance further. You see, our mentors know that we should never be comfortable, and when we are, it is time to change something. Once a plan has been set for our studies, network building, promotion, sales growth, etc., they provide accountability to ensure we stick to the plan.

Like with anything, a relationship with a mentor may not last if it's abused. If you are disinterested in communicating and constantly fail to follow through, you will lose your mentor(s), and as a result your G.A.S., halting your progress. You cannot depend on someone outside of yourself to do all of the work. You must have the drive within you to chase your goals full-on. A mentor sees that special something in you at the very start and merely grooms and coaches you to be all that you can be. See Code R: Roll Up Your Sleeves to read more about drive and hard work.

Support

Work, studies, home life, and even networking can become overwhelming at times. When this happens, a mentor is there to tell us that it is to be expected and okay to feel overwhelmed at times. Some may even provide tips on how to conquer stress and exhaustion based on their own experiences. They know that the road to Luckieville is not an easy one and try to do all that they can to keep us trucking.

Now you may be wondering, with all of the effort that mentors put in, what do they get out of the relationship? They get the satisfaction of helping another individual succeed. They know all about Code G: Give Graciously. It is their hope that you will soon be able to mentor another, creating a ripple effect. Could you imagine what the world would be like if everyone had a Luckie mentor? I get chills just thinking about it and Louis Armstrong's "What a Wonderful World" begins playing in my head.

How to Apply Code M:
Mentors Are a Power Source in Daily Life

People probably do not walk through your city or town with a sign around their neck stating, "I'm a mentor—pick me to help you!," so you may be wondering just how this all works. Oh, how much easier life would be if things worked this way, but as we all know, great things worth having usually do not come this effortlessly. There are many ways to find a mentor, all of which will require a bit of work on your part.

The most common way to find a mentor is through the development of your networks. As you attend events that are of interest to you and that allow you to mingle on a professional level, such as conferences, networking events, company parties, promotional events, etc., you are bound to find many individuals who have a higher level of expertise and/or experience regarding a subject or field than you do. For instance, if you're an amateur photographer looking to become a professional (or even a professional who wants to be better), you may find your mentor at a popular bridal fair or modeling event. If currently working a 9–5 as a business professional and looking to escape the rat race and create your own business, you may find a successful individual at a trade show who can mentor you.

This is not to say that mentors can only be found at organized professional events rather than at a grocery store or trendy hangout, but simply that there is an abundance of potential candidates found at such events and the likelihood of identifying them as suitable mentors is higher. As you may expect, finding people who could be suitable mentors is not enough; you must interact with them. Which conveniently brings us to the next important matter—preparedness. Always be prepared. Present yourself well, ensuring that you are dressed the part and neatly groomed, and be equipped to introduce yourself, make small talk, and exchange business cards. Keep it professional at all times.

I suggest not asking individuals on the spot, the very first time you meet, if they would like to be your mentor. That's because they do not yet know you or your capabilities well enough to know if you have what it takes to be a great mentee. Likewise, you do not know them well. Sure, you may have stalked their LinkedIn profile and know they are qualified, but that does not mean that you are a great fit for each other. As a result, to come off the bat asking such a serious question may come across as unprofessional to some individuals and may very well put the both of you in an awkward position when they have to kindly decline. Although there is a possibility that if you ask the first time you meet they may very well accept, there is also a chance that if they do accept you will find out later that although they may be excellent in their field, they are poor teachers and unable to pass on their knowledge and experience effectively. They may not know the first thing about being a mentor, and as a result, be unable you provide the G.A.S. that you need to succeed as a Luckie. For this reason I ask that you take the time to develop a relationship. Send a follow-up email after you meet. Find out more about them and tell them more about yourself.

Once you feel comfortable that the two of you have enough in common, that your personalities are a good match, and that the person has mentored before (or is a great teacher willing to learn the ropes of mentorship along the way), fire away! Muster up the courage and tell them how honored you are for them to have taken the time out to communicate with you over the last couple of days (or weeks or months) and ask if they would be willing to do so on a more frequent basis through mentorship. Be sure to show your enthusiasm for the possibility; this shows ambition. The worse that they could say is no (likely due to already juggling such a hectic schedule)—and because it will be via email or over the phone it'll be a lot easier to take (you can thank me later for saving you the embarrassment at a public event). Even after a decline, however, keep the door of communication open and be polite. They may refer you to someone more suitable, or at the very least you have made a new connection, an additional link in your network, who may prove very useful to you in the future.

If they do accept—great. Be sure not to stand them up if they invite you for lunch or coffee. Invite them if they do not invite you. Tell your new mentor your long and short-term goals, and allow them to help you to come up with a plan to reach the targets set. Follow through with that plan and continue building the relationship, soaking up the knowledge provided through stories of lessons learned. As noted earlier, communication is key. If you reach a hurdle, call up your mentor for advice. If you successfully accomplished something, call them as well to share the great news. Allow them to share in your successes and be your cheerleader to continue on.

"Lucky" for me, the perfect mentor fell right into my lap, or so it would appear. When I was accepted into an 18-month management training program, I was assigned a mentor, a vice president at the firm. She and I hit it off immediately and she was an excellent mentor, having done it many times successfully in the past. She showed me the ropes of the industry, encouraged me to begin and complete my professional designation (which I did within two years and finished with a distinction—yay!), questioned me regularly regarding the progress of my goals, and introduced me to many influential people along the way. Through her, I found my second mentor, a friend of hers who offered to be my mentor the first time I met him, and a life coach who happened to be my mentor's twin sister who had recently completed a coaching program and started coaching on the side of her career.

For someone on the outside looking in, this may appear as a "lucky coincidence" or as if I was "set up" for success without any effort on my part. What isn't seen, however, is the hard work that it took for me to get into the program, as well as my continued efforts after I got in. I made sure to nourish the mentor relationship provided: If my mentor didn't contact me, I took the initiative to call or write her. I never missed a date and ensured that we caught up frequently. I followed much of her advice, and although the mentorship was for an eighteen-month period, five years later she is still my mentor, and now also a very dear friend. Sometimes things don't work out as we think they should; oftentimes they work out a lot better. I'm a balloon full of optimism, in case you have yet to figure this out. I have found that because I constantly expect the best, I often receive nothing less. This has proved true with my mentor relationship and in many other areas in my life. For this I am truly grateful, and I wish the same for you.

Because We Cannot Leave without a Few Good Quotes

"Mentoring is a brain to pick, an ear to listen, and a push in the right direction."

– John C. Crosby

"Mentors are not there to make us 'happy.' They are there to guide us to the best of their ability."

– Samira DeAndrade

"Your mentors in life are important, so choose them wisely."

– Robert Kiyosaki

"The quintessential mentor is one who shares wisdom and knowledge with the mentee to help improve the mentee."

– Steven B. Greenberg

"The biggest difference is in the leadership. It was better for us. We had more coaches and mentors to help us. A lot of the younger players today suffer from lack of direction."

– Isaiah Thomas

CODE N

NETWORK... THEN NETWORK SOME MORE

Network. A word in itself that has so much power. Growing up, I always heard the phrase, "It isn't what you know, it's who you know." As I've gotten older, I have come to realize that although that statement is not completely accurate—knowledge is a force to be reckoned with and cannot be dismissed completely—who you know is very important. Not unlike a linked group of computer systems working together, a network of people linked together, interacting to exchange services, information, and contacts, will assist you to grow in your career or on your entrepreneurial path.

Without a great network, you cannot be the greatest version of yourself—the Luckie you are destined to be. I cannot emphasize enough how your potential is multiplied when paired with a winning team of individuals around you. Although we can master certain things, we cannot be the expert on everything under the sun, and for that reason, we need to grow our network in order to succeed in life. You may be a great accountant, but a horrible speller. You may be great at sales, but what good is that if you are horrible at saving? You may be one of the best football players in the world, but worthless at branding yourself. Even an awesome doctor can't give herself open-heart surgery. We need to learn from others and, more importantly, begin using their expertise where appropriate.

Building a network is much like attending a farmers' market.

Just as we sift through the produce to find the best avocado to make guacamole, we must too sift through the people that cross our paths and make memorable connections with the ones that are the best fit for our recipe of success. Just as we wouldn't want a bad avocado in our guacamole, we do not want someone who is horrible at their job to be our resource. Therefore, we must seek out those who are the best in their fields along with those just beginning who show promising potential. Once we find them, we then must make it our mission to get to know them.

When it comes to building a network, simply knowing a lot of really great people is never enough. We must be able to contact them at the drop of a hat, to be able to provide a service or product that is equally as beneficial to them, and—seemingly the most obvious—they must know who we are. This means that when we meet up with them again we need to make sure that we have their most up-to-date contact information and leave a memorable, positive impression. Robert Kiyosaki, real estate guru and author of Rich Dad Poor Dad and other best-selling titles, says, "Your network determines your net worth." With that wisdom in mind, we should be motivated to create the best network possible.

How to Apply Code N:
Network... Then Network Some More in Daily Life

Building a great network takes time. Having a drawer filled with business cards is useless if the individuals don't know who you are. You must nurture your professional relationships and should aim to provide a product or service to them that's equally as beneficial as what you would expect to receive from them. Unlike mentorship, networking requires a lot of give and take. Here are a few tips to get you started.

Attend Networking Events and Socialize

This may seem like an obvious suggestion, but the truth is that many people avoid situations where there are a lot of unknown people that they are forced to interact with. I know because I was one of those people. I didn't see the point of "rubbing shoulders." I thought of it as kissing up to people so they will be your friend. In fact, it seemed fake to me. I quickly learned, however, that networking is the game of business and life in general, and that if I didn't play, I would get left behind. Once I began attending, I noticed that there wasn't anything phony about these events at all. There were, of course, people attending that were a little "extra," but I'm sure you could name a few off the top of your head that you interact with on a daily basis that are over the top in any situation. These events were no different.

My coach once gave me an assignment to attend an upcoming networking event and interact with people I didn't know. Okay, that's easy, I thought; she'd never know whether I talked to anyone new. But she then advised that I had to collect 10 business cards by the end of the night and follow up with at least five of them within 24 hours for coffee! If you could only imagine my horror. I don't even drink coffee! As much as I love to talk, I am an introvert by nature, so this assignment definitely required me to step outside of my comfort zone. When I got there I began talking to people right away to get it over and done with. I began noticing that people are quite friendly at these events and easy to talk to. I collected my 10 business cards, followed up with five—and I have never looked back since. I learned the importance of the 24-hour rule. If it's your first time meeting these people, if you wait longer than that they may forget who you are (especially if cocktails were involved)! You cannot afford for this to happen. That and it's just common courtesy. Following up within a day's time shows that you are interested in making a genuine connection and appreciate their time.

Travel

Thanks to social media and technology in general, this world is shrinking at a rapid pace. It is now much easier to know and do business with people in other parts of the globe. Gone are the days of carrier pigeons, fax machines, and handwritten notes. We now have email, video conferencing, and LinkedIn. Even with these advances, however, nothing beats face-to-face meetings, shaking hands, and being in the same space to look a person in the eyes. For this reason, I encourage all who can to travel. Attend overseas conferences that interest you, and when you go on vacation, be conscious of the networking opportunities available.

Other Ways

Everywhere is a networking opportunity if you approach the situation with tact and take the lessons in Code D: Dress for Success to heart. Always be ready to introduce yourself, and have business cards with you at all times. The key is to sell yourself in such a way that they feel that you will be a great person to have in their network. Practice small talk—learn to list your accomplishments without bragging, be sure to listen to the other person (this is so important!), ask questions about what they do, and be prepared to speak about what you currently do or have done in the past. If you can keep someone talking, it's a good sign. The best networkers listen more than they talk, and they always remember to follow up with the connections that they would like to keep!

Another Great Quote from Robert Kiyosaki to Motivate You to Use This Code

"The richest people in the world look for and build networks, everyone else looks for work."

– Robert Kiyosaki

Let's Reinforce with One from Me for Good Measure

"I didn't see the point of 'rubbing shoulders' . . . I quickly learned, however, that networking is the game of business and life in general, and that if I didn't play, I would get left behind."

– Gayneté Edwards

— — —

CODE O

OWN YOUR TRUTH

One of the most difficult lessons to put into practice on the road to Luckieville is to accept ourselves for who we are, and to accept that not everyone will like us. Luckies realize that in order to successfully get on with their lives, they must eliminate the fear of rejection and get comfortable with ruffling feathers along the way. As long as we are authentic and have pure intentions, the opinions of others should not matter. One of my favorite quotes of all time is by Winston Churchill: "You will never reach your destination if you stop and throw stones at every dog that barks." It speaks volumes to me. If we stop and entertain the naysayers along the way—or worse, never begin following our heart out of fear of not being liked—we halt our own progress and waste our energy feeding something that does not serve our highest good.

The great thing about authenticity is that it cannot be stolen or mocked. You are the only one who thinks and acts the way you do. No matter how hard someone tries, they cannot be you. You are as unique as your fingerprints. Pretending to be someone you are not does not get true supporters, friends, customers, or fans, and then when the real you shines through (and believe me, it will), you will lose that which you have worked so hard to create. If you really want to prosper, you must be true to yourself. With nothing to prove, the only competition that you have is the person who stares back at you in the mirror.

To clarify, to be authentic doesn't mean that we cannot change.

We are constantly evolving. I am not the same person that I was 10 years ago. I have changed for the better through life experiences. Living in a developing country for a year taught me gratitude. Being surrounded by beautiful Venezuelan women with equally stunning hearts helped to shrink my ego and taught me kindness. Being held hostage at gunpoint by Colombian cops taught me the importance of family and showing loved ones that I care. Being a teen mom taught me humility and pushed me to become someone my daughter will grow up to be proud of. I could go on forever here, but I'm sure you catch my drift. Change occurs not just through life experience but through purposeful development—seminars, mentorship, coaching, and the like. Remember Code C: Character Building; we Luckies are constantly looking to create a better version of ourselves.

In contrast, problems arise when we attempt to change ourselves to accommodate the opinions of others. This is not something Luckies do. It is impossible to satisfy everyone because we are all so different. When you are your authentic self, the right people are attracted to you. Those that do have an issue with who you are (or who they perceive you to be) do not matter in the great scheme of things because your life is not a product of others' thoughts but of your own. If you are happy with who you are, that is what's truly important.

When you accept yourself and silence the noise of others, you'll have newfound power. An unstoppable force. This force is the connector for many of the other codes in this book—it invokes the passion to follow your heart without worry or fear, to be grateful for your life as it is at this very moment, to have the courage to network, and to build your character.

How to Apply Code O:
Own Your Truth in Daily Life

To start owning your truth, you must first understand who you are. If you are not quite sure how to answer the question, "Who are you?" try creating a list of your strengths and weaknesses—include personality traits and things that you do well (or don't). Take an honest look at yourself and your circumstances and write what you are proud of. Now take a look at what you are not so proud of and come up with ways to improve these things. Lastly, sum your personality up in one sentence by asking yourself how your loved ones would describe you if you were not around. This is your building block. This is who you are. We are not perfect, and that's okay—we are perfect at being ourselves, though. Own it.

Stop to consider the things that really matter in your life—family, friends, shelter, security, food, etc. Doing this helps put things in perspective. When fears or opinions of others come about, ask yourself if what people have to say about you affects any of the important things on your list. When you see that it doesn't, you'll find the courage to continue on in your truth. It's so liberating!

Affirmations can also help you remain true to yourself. Look in the mirror each morning and remind yourself of who you are and your purpose. Then go on to conquer the day fearlessly.

Code S: Surround Yourself with Solitude can also prove beneficial.

Let's Leave You with Some Quotes Worth Remembering

"I don't have to prove anything to anyone, I only have to follow my heart and concentrate on what I want to say to the world. I run my world."

– Beyoncé

"Though we travel the world over to find the beautiful, we must carry it with us, or we would find it not."

– Ralph Waldo Emerson

· — — ·

CODE P

PRAYER AND SUPPORT TEAMS—DO NOT SKIP THIS ONE!

I know this is a controversial code as not everyone believes in a higher power. I can see my dear atheist friend Lamont rolling his eyes as he reads the title. For those who, like Lamont, do not believe, I ask that you continue reading this; you too may find something to take away from this short yet powerful code.

There is something immensely freeing about giving our cares, worries, and fears to another to bear. Likewise, asking for support when we feel as if we cannot do something on our own is vital to living a Luckie life. Knowing your breaking point does not make you weak; rather, it makes you wise. Whether you go to friends, a family member, or to God in prayer, you will find that getting issues off of your chest and requesting assistance helps you to feel better and often opens a world of great possibilities that you were unable to see prior to unloading your troubles.

I have found prayer to be very powerful; answers and solutions present themselves to me in many different ways following a heartfelt prayer. I give thanks for all of my blessings on a daily basis and pray for guidance regularly, even though, with the exception of weddings and funerals, I do not attend church.

I also turn to loved ones when I want a physical shoulder to rest my head on or ears to listen. Comfort is found in knowing that we have someone to turn to in tough times and to celebrate in our victories. For this reason, building a positive support team is so important. Sports teams do not have cheerleaders simply because they are easy on the eyes. They motivate them to win! Family and friends are great resources to use. Be sure to share your fears, goals, and dreams with supportive loved ones. They will quickly become your own personal cheerleaders, motivating you on the road to Luckieville.

How to Apply Code P:
Prayer and Support Teams in Daily Life

I'm not an expert prayer or a very religious person by any means, but that does not stop me from doing it, as I still believe. With a pure heart and my intentions clear, I simply close my eyes and get to it. I always begin by first giving thanks—sincerely. When I do ask for solutions, guidance, or anything else for that matter, I ask for it for the greater good of all concerned. In other words, I want everyone involved to benefit. None of my prayers are identical, and what works for me may not work for you. I will say, however, that practice makes perfect. Get into a habit of giving thanks daily—I find that we already know all too well how to ask for help. Pray in good times and in bad, and you'll likely find that the good times far outweigh the bad.

Open up to loved ones. If they ask how you're doing or what you've been up to, don't just answer with a "fine" or "nothing much." Answer them genuinely. Return the favor and be their support team as well. Getting lucky is a team sport. We must help each other in this endeavor.

Prayer from a Respectable Luckie

"As far back as I can recall, my prayer has been the same: 'Use me, God. Show me how to take who I am, who I want to be and what I can do, and use it for a purpose greater than myself.'"

– Oprah Winfrey

— — . —

CODE Q

QUESTION YOURSELF DAILY

A habit I have found that many Luckies have in common is ending the day by recalling how the day went. Questioning how any part of our day could have been handled better and what we will do differently the next day creates internal dialog that is essential for growth. It is a great practice to hold ourselves accountable for our own actions. We begin to slowly mold ourselves into who we want to be—better versions of who we already are—and therefore better conduits of "luck."

No one is perfect. We can get impatient with our kids, forgetting that what they are saying and doing is perfectly appropriate for their age. We may be holding on to something that happened earlier on in the day and give someone a piece of our mind who may not have really deserved it. Or we may simply not have given our all at a particular task, while knowing that we are capable of so much better. The key is to learn from each mistake made. To grow. And what better way than replaying the day and assessing our actions?

The mere thought of questioning yourself may make you a bit leery—after all, we've always been cautioned that talking to ourselves is the first sign of insanity. Do not fret! This process does not have to happen aloud if you are too afraid of someone overhearing you. I once saw a tee shirt that read, "I talk to myself because sometimes I need expert advice." Bingo. We are the experts on ourselves. Who knows you—your fears, your goals, your triumphs, your struggles—better than you? Therefore, who is better qualified to question your actions than you are?

Sometimes, before the day is even over, I find myself asking questions. If I get offended by something someone says, I always bring it back, asking myself why it bothered me so much. I aim to figure out what my trigger was and how I can release my attachment to it. I am not too proud to admit that I have a pretty quick tongue, and at times I find myself responding to situations that didn't deserve my immediate reaction. I find myself having to step back and ask why I felt the need to say what I did, when and how I said it. I then make a conscious effort to remember that silence is often the best response and to not take things personally. All of this occurs in my head, of course—but the result is the same, a deeper understanding of who I am and what makes me tick. Questioning, and understanding, my emotions and intentions allows me to control my actions and thoughts, which then makes it possible to control my destiny and, ultimately, my luck.

How to Apply Code Q:
Question Yourself Daily in Daily Life

Start by replaying your day in your head each evening. Excluding everyone else, analyze what you did well and what you could have done better. Do not use this as a tool to punish yourself; rather, see it as a way to build yourself up. In other words, if you did more not-so-great things than you would have liked, focus on how to improve the next day rather than sulk about it, thinking you're a monster. Perfection is for robots—and they're so stiff. I prefer the human life.

Play a game to ensure that your daily good deeds far outweigh your actions that could have been handled better. Tip: If you want to win this game, try to avoid gossip. Play naive like you don't know what the gossiper is talking about, ignore them, or change the subject—they'll get the picture. I do this quite well. It doesn't get you a whole lot of friends, but it does get you the right ones.

Quote This One

"No one remains quite what he was when he recognizes himself."
– Thomas Mann

CODE R

ROLL UP YOUR SLEEVES

Making a list of our goals is the easy part. The follow-through on the plans set—that's where we oft encounter our biggest challenge on the road to success. We can read all the motivational quotes that we want, but we have to have that mental fortitude, and be willing to get our hands dirty. If that ambition, that drive to succeed in life, is not within us, we will never be a Luckie. We must be willing to roll up our sleeves and get to work.

If you have read this far, I think it is safe to say that you have the drive and a real interest to succeed. Congratulations; you are one of the few. Now—just what are you going to do to ensure that you do thrive? Work your butt off and follow the codes in this book, of course. Effort is as effort does. Even in the rare instances where people win millions in the lottery, effort is involved. They must take a leap of faith, sacrifice their hard-earned dollar, and go to the store to purchase the winning ticket. Absolutely no "luck"—even that which appears effortless—will occur without some work on your part.

"Luck" is a magnet—one that is attracted to positivity and hard work. Both are required in equal proportions. This book is already dripping with positivity, so now with this code it's time to get down to the nitty-gritty—rolling up your sleeves and getting to work. Lucky for you (pun intended), the average person is lazy. This means you can easily stand out from the crowd by doing just a bit more than is expected of you. Take this a little further, and go beyond the call of duty, and you have distanced yourself substantially. To win in life, you must put in the hard work, long before the prize you wish for appears. For an author, it takes months (or often years) slaving over their words before they ever reach an audience. For an athlete, it is the work put in during the off season that sets them apart during the actual games. Muhammad Ali once said, "The fight is won or lost far away from witnesses—behind the lines, in the gym, and out there on the road, long before I dance under those lights." We must be willing to sacrifice our time, our bodies, our sleep, our social lives to succeed. We often just see the final result of someone's hard work and think he or she is simply born that way. Very seldom is this the case. Even the most gifted of us will be overtaken by the hardest workers at some point. Michelangelo was quoted saying, "If people knew how hard I worked to gain my mastery, I would not seem so wonderful at all." Everyone wants the glory, but very few are willing to roll up their sleeves for the cause. But not you—you will be one of the few.

How to Apply Code R:
Roll Up Your Sleeves in Daily Life

Once you know what it is that you want to do/be, do whatever it takes to get there, and then some. Study the industry/art/market like your life depends on it—because it does. Set yourself apart from the crowd by working and studying your craft harder than you ever have before. Make up your mind that no one and nothing will stop you. Study others who do it well via Google and YouTube. Practice. Practice. Practice.

You must be willing to roll up your sleeves today, right this moment, and for as long as it takes to get to where you wish to be. You must give your all, your very best effort; nothing less will do. Doing this, you cannot fail. This is huge—remember, you cannot fail. Not in the long run, anyway, because you've made up your mind not to give up until you have achieved what you set out to accomplish.

Having the focus to put your head down to work hard at your dreams and not look up until you have succeeded says a lot about you. It shows courage, perseverance, and strength. (All the attributes of a Luckie.) It may be a scary thought if you don't enjoy working hard, but what's scarier is not living to your full potential, leading a mediocre life when you are here to shake this world for the better. We all have a purpose—let's pursue it together.

Hard-Work Quotes to Live By

"Dreams are lovely. But they are just dreams. Fleeting, ephemeral, pretty. But dreams do not come true just because you dream them. It's hard work that makes things happen. It's hard work that creates change."

– Shonda Rhimes

"Talent is never enough. With few exceptions, the best players are the hardest workers."

– Magic Johnson

"If you've been working towards something for five years, I'd say you have a goal in mind. You've probably focused on that goal. Hopefully you've been diligent in pursuing it. If your work pays off, which it most likely will, people might say you're just lucky. Maybe so, because you're lucky enough to have the brains to work hard!"

– Donald Trump

"I've always worked very, very hard, and the harder I worked, the luckier I got.

– Alan Bond

CODE S

SURROUND YOURSELF IN SOLITUDE

Each morning, I wake up extra early to simply sit in silence. You may be thinking, "Well, what's the sense of that? Just spend the moment sleeping in silence." But you see, as important as sleep is, it is no substitute for this code. When I wake up, I take a look at my vision board with excitement and feel myself accomplishing each thing on it. I then close my eyes, clear my mind of the many things on the agenda for the day, and simply breathe. It is my moment of clarity. In silence, many answers are found and true relaxation occurs. With all of the work that you will be putting in, and all of the people that you will be meeting on your road to Luckieville, spending at least five minutes a day in silence is essential to your mental health.

Many hear the word meditation and shudder; they have preconceived notions of someone who meditates wearing a high turban, with their legs crossed, in the middle of nowhere, with incense burning around them, humming in a tune that is most unusual. Yes, some people do this, and you are welcome to do so as well, if you like—but this is not what I do, nor what we will be looking at in this code. I do not use incense (it makes me choke) nor do I cross my legs like a yogi (too uncomfortable for me) or hum (I cannot take myself seriously when I do). This may change over time, and I'm sure some experienced meditators are cringing at the thought of what I'm about to teach, and that's okay. This is why this code has the word solitude rather than meditation, because by some definitions,

I'm sure this doesn't count as meditation. Well, that and it is Code S, so I needed a word that starts with an s. Nevertheless, we all do things differently, so what works for me may not work for you. The key is to just find a minimum of five minutes a day you can spend by yourself, in a quiet place, to just breathe. The more time you have, the better.

We are often so consumed with the routine of daily life—constantly doing for others—that we begin to slowly lose ourselves. In silence, we find our passions. In silence, we find our peace. No matter what is going on around us, when we are silent and still, everything is in harmony. Silence is the greatest remedy when we are lost; our heart is a compass and works best without interruption. Even if we do not feel lost, at the very least the silence helps to relax us, to collect ourselves, to provide a newfound burst of positive energy that we desperately need to get lucky.

The struggle most people have, and that I too struggled with, is to sit without the mind racing. Practice makes perfect in this regard. When I first began taking a moment of solitude, I started with five minutes and forced myself to sit still. Even though I was sitting still and it was quiet all around me, my mind was running a marathon: What will I make for dinner? What emails will I get in my inbox at work? Am I doing this right? What is supposed to happen? The more I sat in solitude, however, the easier it got. I soon found myself asking more profound questions, such as, What can I do to make a difference? Where do my passions lie? How can I use my passion for change? I began to realize that I could control my thoughts with a little effort and, if I could control them, maybe I could also silence them. It became easier as I continued this practice. I then increased the time I spent in solitude—this was most beneficial! I spent the first few minutes with my deep thoughts, then sat in silence the remainder of the time, enjoying the present moment. I can now sit in complete silence, and oh, what a pleasure it is. No thoughts, no noise—just me breathing.

How to Apply Code S:
Surround Yourself in Solitude in Daily Life

I know that five minutes of silence may be difficult to find, especially if you have children. Scratch that; the idea of even being able to get five minutes to yourself is dang near impossible, right? I know. I've been there, and let me tell you, you need it more than anyone, and you *so* have the time. Here are some ways to find five minutes of silence.

Try locking yourself in the bathroom for five minutes to get some me time. Can't get any peace in there, either? Do not fret; there are other options.

Try going to sleep five minutes earlier, and getting up five minutes earlier. This way, you lose nothing, and have so much to gain. I believe it was Benjamin Franklin who said, "Early to bed, early to rise makes a man healthy, wealthy, and wise."

Not an early riser? If you go to run a quick errand, when you return, instead of rushing back inside, try staying in the car for just five minutes to unwind.

As a last resort, when doing a mindless task—like washing the dishes, for example—put on some headphones and listen to some soothing melodies.

We are all aware of the negative side effects of stress. If stress is a part of your daily life, it is time to do some easy preventative therapy, namely, finding the time to spend in solitude. Whatever it takes, future Luckie, whatever it takes.

When you make spending time in solitude a habit, you will find that you desire more time to enjoy this practice. When this occurs, you may find Oprah and Deepak's 21-Day

Meditation Experience beneficial.

Let's Quote the Expert!

"To make the right choices in life, you have to get in touch with your soul. To do this, you need to experience solitude, which most people are afraid of, because in the silence you hear the truth and know the solutions."

– Deepak Chopra

CODE T

TIME TO CUT FEAR

We may not want to admit it, but fear plagues us all at one point or another in our lives. We worry about what others may think of us, fear if we can actually pull off that huge dream of ours, or whether we will have enough funds left to make it to the next payday. When we don't take action, the fear remains, moving us from a moment of fear to a lifetime of it. Luckies cut fear as soon as it occurs and fearlessly take action toward their desires. The reality is, until we accept fears for what they are—blocks that we create which prevent our growth—make a conscious effort to replace the fearful thoughts with loving ones, and then take action, we will never reach our full potential.

We cannot begin to do something extraordinary by carrying on with our lives as we have in the past—change must occur. Change is the catalyst that jumpstarts a Luckie life. Yet so many of us fear change. It is necessary for us to learn how to transform our fearful thoughts into purposeful, optimistic ones that support what we wish to accomplish. We need to replace thoughts about what scares us with thoughts that motivate us to take action. Ignoring plaguing, fearful thoughts is not enough—like a baby, they will keep crying and get louder as time progresses; we must raise them up and then change them. Then, and only then, will progress be made.

Fear is most apparent in our lives when we are thinking about major life changes. Things like starting a family, getting married, switching careers, or pursuing a lifelong passion put us into panic mode very fast. We have never done it before, so just how do we know we will succeed? What if it isn't what we thought it would be? What if we disappoint someone? What if we fail ourselves? For starters, these thoughts, if persistent, will increase the likelihood of failure. We never know for sure where life will take us once we make up our mind to take action and make a change—but one thing is certain, if we do nothing, we will remain where we have always been, and that thought is much more daunting to me.

I strongly believe that wherever we are in life, and whatever we are doing at this very moment, it is as it should be. Likewise, if a great opportunity for growth presents itself, it is time for change. If we have a chance to follow our hearts, we can never be wrong, for even in failure we have an opportunity for development. Who knows; the lesson learned in that one failure may be just what is needed to prepare for that very large victory waiting around the corner. We will never know, however, if we do not cut our fear and take positive, purposeful action. Too often we allow fear to stop us from reaching our full potential; but not anymore, right, future Luckie?

Dale Carnegie once said, "Inaction breeds doubt and fear. Action breeds confidence and courage. If you want to conquer a fear, don't sit at home and think about it. Go out and get busy." Luckies are forever pushing boundaries and breaking through comfort zones.

How to Apply Code T:
Time to Cut Fear in Daily Life

Fear will creep in from time to time, of that there is no doubt, but the key is to limit its stay in our lives. Let's explore some ways to do just that.

Replacing our fearful thoughts with positive ones is always a great place to begin. This is very easy, as we just think the opposite. Here are a few examples:

Change, "What happens if I fail?" to "What can I expect when I succeed?"

Change, "What if I hate it?" to "What if I absolutely love it?"

Change, "What happens if I don't have enough money?" to "What happens if I get more money than I know what to do with?"

Change, "What happens if I disappoint someone?" to "What if everyone is so proud of me?"

By consciously replacing the negative, fearful thoughts with higher-vibrating positive ones, we begin to raise our spirits and we start to feel better, which puts us in a position to act out of purpose and love, rather than out of fear.

You can also try making a list (yes, I looove my lists) of all the reasons you want to do something. Seeing this in writing may be the only push you need to cut your fear.

Affirmations are also very useful—practice them when fearful. Below are some fear-cutting affirmations to begin, then you can make up your own as you feel fit. Repeat the ones that resonate with you whenever doubt slips into your head.

Affirmations to Cut Fear

"I am capable of whatever I set my mind out to achieve. I surprise myself sometimes with my ability to adapt and soar."

"Fear has no place in my life. I am too busy thinking of the many opportunities I have for success."

"I always make the right decision, and I love that."

"The butterflies in my stomach are my motivation to grow my own wings and fly."

Quotes to Help Motivate You Past Fears

"I have learned over the years that when one's mind is made up, this diminishes fear; knowing what must be done, does away with fear."

– Rosa Parks

"We can easily forgive a child who is afraid of the dark; the real tragedy of life is when men are afraid of the light."

– Plato

"The only thing we have to fear is fear itself."

– Franklin D. Roosevelt

CODE U

USE YOUR RESOURCES

Just as we would put up an umbrella without second guessing when it begins to rain, we must look to utilize that which we have available to us in order to prosper on our road to Luckieville. Why struggle to do everything ourselves, reinventing the wheel, when we have resources available, and people in our networks that are experts at what they do? Why attempt a task through trial and error, when there are countless books and YouTube videos available to assist? The price we pay for the expertise of people in our network, or the cost of a guidebook for that matter, will be small compared to the time wasted trying to do a difficult task ourselves. Time is the most precious resource that we have; we must guard it like a precious jewel, and a great way to begin is by ensuring that we use the other resources available to us.

We have already established that building our networks is vital; a network is useless, however, if you do not utilize your newfound connections. What's the point of having amazing people in your circles, if you do not seize the opportunity to use their knowledge and skills? Like a spider builds a web to catch prey, networks are built to support us and prevent us from falling into the trap of wasting unnecessary time. In return, we pay them for their services (perhaps at a discounted rate) or even at times get a freebie because it is expected that our skillset will be of use to them in the future. Remember, it is all about give and take.

Everyone is always looking for a shortcut on the road to Luckieville. An overnight success route. A get-rich-quick scheme. A "lucky" break. The reality is, there is no such thing. Really. What appears to be an overnight success is a result of many nights' work. Even viral YouTube videos are the result of filming, editing, and sharing, which requires some effort, and the success rarely lasts longer than a couple days. Get-rich-quick schemes fail all the time. What often looks like a "lucky" break is actually the result of the Luckie utilizing many of the codes found in this book, which we know by now takes ongoing effort. Do not lose hope, however, dear reader, because utilizing the codes is not only a surefire way to Luckieville but also very fulfilling—and the time it takes to get there is cut significantly when we utilize our resources.

Allowing someone in our network to introduce us to a Luckie that they are friendly with cuts out a lot of the time it would take for us to get to know this person on our own. If you're rolling up your sleeves to open a new business, you should utilize the expert carpenters, accountants, marketers, etc. in your networks. If short on funds and unable to hire an expert, you should look to utilize the many free online resources available to learn. This will save you a lot of time, errors, and money in the long run. By not taking heed of this important lucky code, you will waste precious moments—moments that could have been used to read something that builds your character, to spend longer moments in solitude, to master your hobbies, or even to come up with a new marketing plan for your business. I cannot stress enough how important it is to save time where possible. We can spend money and then get more money later, but once time is gone, there is no way to recoup it—ever! Right now would be a great time to cue the music to *Jaws* in your head for dramatic effect.

Okay, so now you know that utilizing the people and things around you is important. Now I want you to understand that you should get the help required without feeling guilty about it. We often feel the need to apologize for "being a pain" or "bothering" people. But they are doing their jobs, or have willingly offered to help, so there is no reason to apologize. As long as we are kind and our requests are warranted, it's perfectly fine to request something. After all, it will impact our lives once they complete the job, and they want us to be satisfied. I was reminded of the importance of this when I slipped back into the apologetic phase while working on this book. Yes, I too slip—but quickly recover!

My boyfriend's brother is an awesome graphic designer, Duane Jones of Be Glitterati (how's that for a plug?). He agreed to do my book cover for me—free of charge! How "lucky" is that? This was a huge savings for me, so I felt like I was being a pain requesting that he change the color theme, layout, font, etc. over and over again. And like all people do when they think they are being a pain, I started off every conversation with, "I'm sorry, but can you..." He kindly asked me to stop apologizing and assured me that this is the normal process. He also reminded me that I am perfectly entitled to have it look just the way I envisioned it. Of course it is! Of course I do! I wanted to slap myself for being so silly and needing the reminder to begin with. I didn't ask for a freebie; he offered, and then he professionally carried out the process as if I were paying him. Boy, oh boy, is utilizing resources some sort of amazing.

How to Apply Code U:
Use Your Resources in Daily Life

When you have a project or task, think, "What exactly is it that I will need?" Then make a mental list (or even better, an actual list) of everything required. If there is something on the list that you are not an expert in—get assistance from your network, find support online, or go to a library or bookstore.

If you do not know the first place to begin, consult someone who has already done something similar, or ask Uncle Google. He's wise beyond his years, believe me.

When you do get assistance from someone—and you will (even a babysitter is assistance)—thank them for their help, but do not apologize. Be kind and look to assist them wherever you can. A pure heart can never be faulted. In fact, you'll find that many people want to help you.

I Want to Reinforce This Very Important Message

"The price we pay for the expertise of people in our network, or the cost of a guidebook for that matter, will be small compared to the time wasted trying to do a difficult task ourselves. Time is the most precious resource that we have; we must guard it like a precious jewel, and a great way to begin is by ensuring that we use the other resources available to us."

– Gayneté Edwards

••• ▬

CODE V

VICTORY PERSPECTIVE—TAKE THIS VIEW

Our thoughts and words are time machines to our future. With this in mind, we must proceed with great caution. Don't worry; this can be an awesome thing! If our thoughts are positive and our actions support the optimistic thoughts, we will be victorious on our journey to Luckieville. However, we have to believe that we are "lucky" in order to ever become it. Our perspective, not our circumstances, determines our outcome. In other words, the cards themselves aren't "lucky," we bring "luck" to the cards by how we play the game. Amazing, right?

There have been countless books on this single code alone, The Secret being one of the most popular, and it hasn't sold almost 20 million copies worldwide for nothing! Thoughts are the real deal, and until we grasp and begin implementing this victory perspective, we will be stuck in the loser's circle. Everything is energy; we learned this at a tender age. Many greats of the past have spoken about the power of positive thinking and how it can affect our lives for the better, yet many still see it as some New Age fluke. To the doubters, I say this—what's the harm in trying it out? Positive thinking, that is. I find many fear this concept because if it is true (which it most certainly is), the opposite must also hold true. Negative thought patterns create a nightmare of a life. This is scary, because a lot of people do not know how to think positively. This is where I come in. Code E: Eliminate the Negativity assisted you with conquering the nasty monster of negativity; now we will look at how easy it can be to see victory around every corner, and the lovely benefits of doing so.

I have already touched on a few of my "lucky coincidences," so now let's get into what most people associate with "luck"—the winning of material items. I win everything; I kid you not. If there is a raffle, I walk away with a prize. If there is a bet, I usually come out on top. If buying scratch cards, I always get my money back and then some. Just last month alone, I won an iPad mini, two grocery vouchers totaling $400 (one for $300 and one for $100), and $1,000 in cash! All by exercising my ability to see my victory before it happens. On my first cruise (and the first time I had ever gone into a casino), I won $3,900 on a two-cent slot machine. Yes, you read that correctly! I do not share any of this to brag, but to show you that I'm not writing this book as a spectator of "luck"—I am Lady Luckie herself.

So just how do I do it? Simple—I participate knowing that I will win. Many people participate, but in the same breath used to request the ticket, they mutter, "I don't know why I'm getting this, I never win anything anyway." And you know what? They don't. Participating is not enough, and saying you will win isn't even enough. You must feel it! For the latest raffle I took part in, tickets were $1 and I bought 50 tickets. There were thousands sold, so in the grand scheme of things, my probability of winning still appeared to be quite low, but by purchasing so many, I was committed and my mind was made. "I'm bound to win something—I always do," was my mindset. Not to mention, all proceeds of the raffle were being matched and given to a local charity, so I felt great knowing that I was able to help someone in need. This was a win-win!

I recall looking at the prizes and getting excited thinking about which I wanted to win. The raffle was nearing the end and there were only a few prizes left, but I didn't lose hope. The grocery voucher was mine—I had claimed it as soon as I saw it. When the prize was called off, and they reached into the spinning wheel, I looked at my friend and said, "That's mine." And as the announcer said, "The winner is..." I called my name along with him! The tongue and mind are an amazing combination when used correctly. My friend looked on in shock as I walked up to collect my $300 grocery voucher. Her shock continued when I won another $100 voucher in a separate raffle the very next day.

The same mindset is to be applied for every area of your life—your health, your wealth, your career, and your relationships all begin to flourish with a victory perspective. So why do some people feel such resistance to employing this code? The problem I find is that optimism is often associated with naivety. People believe that if one always sees the sunshine in every situation, they do not use reason or plan for the possibility of the storm. This is baloney. Absolute baloney. Victory thinkers are the kings and queens of reason because they know that their thoughts shape their lives and figure that with this knowledge, it would be irrational not to use it to their benefit. Positive thinking does not mean that you do not understand that some not-so-great things can occur; rather, it means that you believe that the very best outcome will be the end result. With this in mind, you are able to better handle undesirable situations.

How to Apply Code V:
Victory Perspective in Daily Life

For starters, you cannot win without an attempt. It is silly to say that you never win anything if you never enter or put your name forward. It's elementary, future Luckie; you must play to win. And if you put your name forward and do not win right away, do not curse all future chances. No negativity allowed in Luckieville, remember? So from now on, give the next chance to win something a shot—deal?

Next, you must have confidence in your "luck"—yup, before it even happens. You must believe that you are the winner long before the prize arrives. You owe yourself this. Often deep down in those sticky feelings we love to ignore, we feel as though we do not deserve to have something great, erroneously believing that we are not good enough for it. It's time to throw these limiting thoughts away permanently because they do not serve you. You are an amazing, unique individual capable of great feats, and you deserve to live a life you love. You owe yourself the opportunity to partake in things that make you happy and win splendid prizes—because who doesn't like free stuff?

If you have a big interview coming up, prep your butt off and then claim it! Faith in your own abilities is such an important component to winning in life. Sure, the recruiters may have seen some really great candidates prior to your interview, but one thing you know for sure—they did not have you! Let your inner light shine brighter than the Vegas strip and you cannot lose. When you act like a winner, you become one so fast. Victory is yours. I believe in you; now do your part, please, by believing in yourself.

An Affirmation to Use When Doubting Your Abilities

"I am a winner, by every definition of the word. No one has ever been me, and no one will ever be. This alone makes me unique and able to contribute something amazing to this world. The universe appreciates this and rewards me."

CODE W

WINNING PLANS OF PURPOSE

Luckies know that in order to win at life, there must be a plan in place. An end result visualized and mapped out. An ultimate goal that is so large, the mere thought of it sends shivers down our backs because it seems unattainable at times. (But we quickly get over that fear.) We then break down that goal into smaller pieces to make the achievement process a little easier. Even these bite-sized chunks, however, are huge stepping stones out of our comfort zones, stretching us uncomfortably past our set limitations.

The difference between Winning Plans of Purpose and all other plans is that the former are centered around our passions (not money, fame, or anything else). What we are most passionate about gives us huge clues towards our true reason for being—our life's purpose. In order for this plan to be a win-win, our ultimate goal must be grounded in our life's purpose. Then, we focus on rolling up our sleeves and following through on it. Because as we know, a plan is just a road map; it is up to us to follow it.

I created my Winning Plan of Purpose by first identifying my passions. Two of my passions are to assist others to be all that they can be and to write. So for me it was a no-brainer to create a self-help book and a blog. My blog, entitled Goal Chasers: G.A.M.E. Changers (my initials spell "game"—pretty clever, huh?) can be found on my website, www.gaynete.com, where I provide weekly motivational posts, sharing stories of my life with lessons learned along the way and dishing out tips for success. The feedback so far has been phenomenal. My heart swells with joy when I receive a message that my words have assisted someone's current situation and pushed them to do better. I know I am on the right path.

Now here is the wild part—although the book writing process and blog were (and still are) a lot of hard work and have pulled me far out of my comfort zone, they were only my baby steps, my starting point for helping those who need guidance on their way to Luckieville. I have so many other parts to my Winning Plan of Purpose that I am working towards to assist others in chasing their goals! Stepping out of comfort zones and getting uncomfortable is a constant for Luckies. When following your Winning Plan, you will find this to be a constant for you too. Embrace it.

I will soon show you how to create your own Winning Plan of Purpose, however, if you are struggling with finding your way or need a push, do feel free to visit my site and check out my Work With Me page. I don't want you to feel bombarded with information, but I do feel it would be a disservice not to share how I can help you, especially because you could very well benefit tremendously. Finding out where our passions lie and creating a plan can be a daunting task and you shouldn't have to go at it alone. If you need help, know that I'm here for you.

You may not know exactly what it is that you want to do, and that's okay. You may find that the mere dissatisfaction of where you currently are is motivation enough to figure it out and do something great. We all have the potential to do something phenomenal, and if you are reading this book, chances are you know this already and are looking for guidance. Everything works out in divine timing. Your ideas will come in full force once you're ready, and not a moment sooner. Be patient, be open to receive your blessings as they come, and remain passionate about making something of yourself. That inner fuel alone is enough to jump start the preparation for a winning plan.

Having a Winning Plan of Purpose in place is invigorating for our souls and creates a clarity that is unmatched. When we are clear, we take calculated steps for action and are more likely to achieve our goals. When we pair our plan with the other codes in the book, we win big. We change from goal chasers to game changers. We make a difference! These achievements come across as "coincidences" and "lucky breaks" to those on the outside looking in. But we know better now, huh? This thing called "luck" that Luckies seem to have a lot of is all about the choices we make, our intentions, our passion, our desire for success, our work ethic.

How to Apply Code W:
Winning Plans of Purpose in Daily Life

Step 1

As I said before, a Winning Plan is centered around your passion. What is it that you are passionate about? If you could make a living doing anything in the world, what would it be? No buts, ifs, or maybes allowed. What would you do? Take as long as you need to figure this out, because you cannot move on to the next step without an answer to this one. Once you have your answer, please write it down.

Step 2

Now that you are clear on your passion, what steps can you take right now to get you to a point where you can live out that passion? Do you need further education? Do you need new connections? More money? All of the above? Great, that's a start. Write out your Winning Plan requirements then break them into steps, noting how you will achieve them. If your answer is "It's just not possible" or "There's no way I could ever do it," then work on increasing your confidence. We spoke about fear already and know how detrimental it can be to a lucky life. Lack of confidence is in the same boat. Remember, absolutely anything is possible. A coach or mentor can assist you in working through fear and increasing your confidence. You could even pop on by to my blog for some motivation and inspiration to push you through the slump. Excuses are tools used by individuals who have fears stronger than their passions. Do not let fear paralyze you. Seek that which you require and do not accept no as an answer—not even from yourself—when pursuing your goals.

Step 3

Work your behind off in a frenzy to complete that first step on your list. Then the next. And so forth until you reach that ultimate goal. Whether it be a month or five years—do not stop until you get that which you desire. Even ten years is trivial when you stop to think how long you've been working without passion. Do not give up. I really want you to follow through with this, so I've created a Winning Plan cheat sheet just for you. It provides an outline, examples, and an empty template to help you to easily pull all of the pieces of this three-step process together to create the ultimate Winning Plan of Purpose. If this sounds like something that would be helpful, simply go to www.gaynete.com, subscribe to my mailing list, and then click on the Contact tab. Send me a message stating, "Lucky Code Reader and fellow Goal Chaser—Can I have the Winning Plan Cheat Sheet?" and I will email it off to you. This is a secret offer made only to you, my reader, so please do not share.

Breakdown

To provide you with an example, let's say your answer to Step 1 is to be a television anchor. You have no idea how to begin, but figure you may need a little more education and need to get noticed because you are from a small town. You're halfway through Step 2! If you cannot afford to quit your day job and head off to school, make a list of all the ways you can make this happen: look for scholarships online and apply for all of them, save up some money and take online courses. Remember the Victory Perspective from the last code? Apply it.

The getting noticed bit is much easier, thanks to social media. Create a new Instagram account or Facebook page and begin learning all about the best marketing techniques for them, because you are essentially marketing yourself. There are many people offering free webinars on the subject. You could even begin making short video clips reporting happenings around your town. The possibilities are endless.

Another step could be to begin working at a local news station. Go there (applying Code D: Dress for Success, of course) and see what positions are available. If you present yourself well enough, you may even convince them to create an intern position. Sometimes starting from the bottom (insert Drake's catchy "Started from the Bottom" song here) is the very best thing for you. You must be willing to sacrifice something temporarily (like money, by way of a pay cut or investment in your education) for something much bigger in the future (living your dream). Do not give up.

Inspiration to Keep Going

Did you know that Walt Disney was turned down over 300 times when applying to banks for a loan to begin building his theme park? Imagine all the joy and creativity the world would have missed out on if he had given up on his dreams due to setbacks or failures. Now if that doesn't inspire you to keep going, I don't know what will!

CODE X

JUMP HURDLES (CASE IN POINT)

When on a huge mission like shaking the world, chasing your dreams, and getting "lucky" in life (which is why you are reading this book after all, right?), hurdles are bound to appear. Yup, there's no escaping them. The trick isn't learning how to avoid them, but how to overcome them, jumping them one by one as they appear and learning a valuable lesson along the way. Luckies are often praised for their success and asked just how they did it—once they make it, of course. Prior to that, they are usually asked just why they are doing something so risky. I have not heard a success story yet that didn't include some difficulty the person had to overcome, and believe me, I have had my fair share as well. See, here's the thing: we do not start out where we want to be; we must work to get there. Along the way, there will be trials that can wear you down if you allow them to. But Luckies simply do not allow those trials to defeat them; they in fact use them to grow.

A simple example of eliminating a hurdle is when I reached the letter x in my book outline. I had a difficult time coming up with a code that Luckies use that starts with x. I refused to let it defeat me, however, and through that mindset alone, I figured it out. No matter what comes up (or, in some cases, what doesn't happen), know that there is always a way around (or over) it. Throughout this book, I've said that there are no excuses for not reaching your dreams and that every problem has a solution—and I believe it wholeheartedly. Nothing can stop us from achieving our goals once we make up our minds that we will get there no matter what. One guarantee we have is that if we stop, we will never get there, so we must continue to push on.

The late, great Dr. Martin Luther King Jr. once said, "If you can't fly then run, if you can't run then walk, if you can't walk then crawl, but whatever you do, you have to keep moving forward." I just love this quote. How we get there will vary, and we may not hop over hurdles in daily life as gracefully as an Olympic medalist, but we will get there if we make up our minds to never quit. We may stumble as we reach a hurdle, but stumbles are a part of life and assist with our development; we must get up and continue on, knowing that our dreams are more important than the scrapes and bruises obtained along the way. The next time we will be prepared and better able to hop that hurdle.

How to Apply Code X:
Jump Hurdles in Daily Life

The key to jumping any hurdle you encounter in life is to always remember that your purpose is much bigger than your problem. This way, you begin looking for solutions, instead of stressing over causes.

Use Code P: Prayer and Support Teams. Knowing you have someone on your side in a difficult situation is a true blessing, but do not forget to use Code P in the good times as well!

Roll up your sleeves and get to work on your goal. Work on another piece of your Winning Plan of Purpose until you figure out how to jump the part with the hurdle. And know that you will find a way.

Sleep on it. Many times a hurdle appears larger than it actually is because we have something else going on when we encounter the problem and cannot focus on it with a clear mind. A well-rested, fresh brain can give a better perspective. You can even use Code S: Surround Yourself in Solitude. Sometimes all we need is a little space and silence to get clear on what needs to be done.

Make a mental note of the hurdle and any warning signs you may have overlooked. Next time, you just may be able to catch a similar issue before it arises. Do not be discouraged. Find the lesson in the hurdle and count your blessings—it could always be worse.

Quote-Worthy—I Like How He Thinks

"Life's problems wouldn't be called 'hurdles' if there was not a way to get over them."

– Noel C. Gill

— · — —

CODE Y

YES MEN QUICKLY BECOME TRASH CANS

Luckies know the power of their choices and value their time dearly; therefore, they do not accept every offer that comes their way or agree to every request asked of them. If you want to be a Luckie, you must follow suit and learn to put your foot down when needed. If you say yes to everything asked of you, when you really want to say no, you will find yourself quickly becoming a trash can for the work that others don't want to do for themselves. This is not going to get you where you want to go, future Luckie. Time to nip this in the bud now!

A question is phrased as a query for a reason—you control the response. Do not be afraid of saying no when you are unable or unwilling to complete a task. To take on more than you can handle and nosedive, or to do something halfheartedly because you just aren't interested, is so much worse than denying the request to begin with. Doing anything less than your best work is a bad reflection of you and what you are capable of producing. Guard your brand—your reputation, your image—very closely. When you produce only the best and take on only that which you desire, an occasional, well-intentioned no will never turn the right people away.

Courage is a mighty virtue and needed in heavy doses on the road to Luckieville. To be a Luckie, you must have the courage to say no; you simply cannot go through life giving everyone what they want and ignoring your own desires. Of course, this doesn't relate to tasks on your job description. If your boss comes over and asks you to do something (that you know you are supposed to do), they are just being polite—although phrased as a question, it is really a command. Your boss may just need a lesson in assertiveness.

In this code we are referring to the things that you *really* don't want to do and that you have a right to say no to: The request to pick something up for someone when you know your busy schedule will not allow for it without missing something important you have to do. The invitation to work extra hours when you have already made plans with your family. The bid to help someone who doesn't want to help themselves. The offer to work for a company that looks great on paper, but isn't where your heart is. The plea from a friend to borrow some more money when you know you will not get it back (especially if you do not have money to spare without the guarantee that it will be returned). The request to help someone at your job who takes the credit for your hard work every time you assist without as little as a "thank you." The invitation to the wedding of an acquaintance you aren't very fond of. Do not feel guilty for putting down your foot and saying no. If you do not, you will get walked on and known as the yes man (yup—even if you're a woman). You will keep getting unwanted requests until you start saying no. Like a trash can, you will not be respected and will become the common place for waste. Wasted time. Wasted efforts. Wasted resources. What you see as your kindheartedness will be continually taken advantage of if you allow it.

How to Apply Code Y:
Yes Men Quickly Become Trash Cans in Daily Life

To make things crystal clear here, the tasks we refer to in this code are favors asked of you by others that will neither make nor break a situation—if you decline, someone else will be asked, or the person will do it his or herself. This is not to be confused with Code G: Give Graciously, where we do for others in need out of the compassion in our hearts without expecting anything in return. Got it?

When asked to do something/go somewhere/accept something and you think your saying yes may be taken for granted, ask yourself the following questions.

Do I really want to do this, or do I simply not want to ruffle feathers here?

If the latter, politely decline or make a mental note to do it this one time and decline the next time around. Then stick to it. Real friends and people who have your best intentions at heart will not be offended.

Will doing this assist me in some way, or will it further delay what I have planned to do?

It is not selfish to consider the implications doing a favor for someone will have on your own plans. This question should not be the sole reason for agreeing to or denying a task, but needs to be deliberated.

Have I been asked this before and didn't want to do it the last time but did it anyway?

If the same person is asking the same the question and you did it last time and didn't enjoy it, why say yes again? You are being set up as a trash can, honey; say no before they grab that bag.

Commit to quit. Say no and mean it.

If I decline, can anyone else do this task?

We all love to think we are the only ones who can do something, but if you decline, is it possible that the individual asking will go right along trucking to ask the next person, or are you truly their only hope? It's less likely that they have no other options and more likely that you are just the easiest to get over.

If I accept, will it be appreciated?

We all love to feel appreciated. Come on, admit it. Will the person asking appreciate your willingness to assist or do they treat it as an obligation? If an obligation, it's time for a heart to heart. Find the courage to respectfully say what is on your mind.

Affirmations to Assist the Yes Man Trash Can

"Today I will say what I mean and mean what I say, knowing that a well-intentioned 'no' can never get in my way. All that I do and all that I don't is for my greater good. All is well, all the time."

"My success is not defined by my ability to agree and accept, rather by considerations and choices made—and I make great choices every time."

— — · ·

CODE Z

ZERO TO HERO? REMAIN HUMBLE

You will likely note a rapid change in your circumstances as soon as you begin implementing the codes found in this book. This is great news—celebrate, share the codes with others, change the world, and give Oprah a hug for me—but remember, through it all, to remain humble. Ever watched a game show where someone has it all and gets a little too cocky? You begin getting uncomfortable just watching the shenanigans, knowing it will soon come to an end. The winnings slip away pretty fast, huh? The same goes with our "luck." Being modest is an admirable trait that most Luckies share.

The reality is, people don't like arrogant, conceited individuals. I know because I was one. I was young and immature and had no idea the damage I was doing. I thought that because I was walking down runways and appearing in local magazines, I was the cat's meow. I didn't realize I was being conceited (do we ever?)—until I was elected Most Conceited in my high school yearbook. A local retailer also refused to work with me because of my arrogant attitude. Punch. In. The. Stomach. Thank God for reality checks. That same year I became an exchange student. I lived in Venezuela for eleven months, and to this day I am convinced it was the universe's plan to get my ego in check. The women there were drop-dead gorgeous—every single one of them. For the first time, I felt inadequate. What shocked me more than their extraordinary outer beauty, however, was their inner beauty; they were kind and generous.

What did I have to offer? "Looks fade with time," I thought to myself. What a soul-shaking moment. It was then that I realized looks mean very little and what is beautiful to one is hideous to another. Looks may get you where you want to go, but kindness and humility will keep you there. I committed to change my ways. I threw away my handheld mirror and began focusing on enhancing my personality instead.

It is so easy for us to get caught up in the hype of winning that we forget that it is a blessing that we should remain grateful for. But just as easy as it comes, it can be taken away. That's why this code reminds you to stay humble when going from "zero to hero." If you show gratitude, pray, help others, and remain the sweetheart you were all along, you will find more "luck" will continue to flow your way and you will be better liked for it too, which is always a plus when on the road to Luckieville. Who will want to be in your network if all you do is talk about yourself all the time and "big up" all that you have? I'll give you a clue here—absolutely no one. Even if you commit to changing your ways, the people you rubbed the wrong way will not forget it and are unlikely to give you another chance. Only recently did the retailer who refused to work with me all those years ago begin warming back up to me. Save yourself the headache and heartache by remaining humble and being true to yourself. If your true self is naturally arrogant, I ask you to go to Code C: Character Building and work on building a better version of yourself. Not only will you have an easier time navigating your way to Luckieville, you will be a better person for it.

How to Apply Code Z:
Zero to Hero? Remain Humble in Daily Life

We are here on this Earth to make a difference. Sometimes, along the way, we get recognized in a big way. Becoming a "hero" can sometimes make us feel very important, which we are. All of us are. The issue arises when we believe we are more important than those around us. Self-reflection is in order when this occurs.

Humbleness is quite the difficult code to teach, as it truly comes from within. You will find, however, that the other codes in this book (namely, C, G, I, J, P, S, and Q) call for a humble spirit. Practice them often and you will shape your world into an awesome place where your dreams come true. You will become your own version of a "hero" and keep your humility intact.

Journaling about your daily thoughts and about the day's interactions may also be of some assistance. It doesn't have to be a novel, just a few sentences, then review your writings on a monthly basis. It is easier to identify undesirable, egotistical traits/tendencies/thoughts on paper.

If you were intrigued by my personal story in this code, or it struck a cord, I encourage you to head on over to my blog, where I dive into much deeper detail about it. It is my hope that through sharing my story, you too can grow and learn to shrink your ego.

A Quote to Put It All in Perspective

"Climb the mountain so you can see the world, not so the world can see you."
– David McCullough Jr.

LUCKIEVILLE WRAP-UP

By now you will have figured out that becoming a Luckie isn't in the charms you carry or how lucky your parents are, but rather how you spend your time and the choices you make. One of the most important choices to make on this new journey is refusing to settle. Do not mistake comfort for happiness. Too often we settle when there is still so much potential for us to grow... to prosper. Fear is a huge contributor to this stalemate.

If you find yourself hesitating to change your daily routine and to follow the codes that will help you, out of fear that you will fail, I want you to remember this: you cannot fail on the path to self-improvement (even your stumbles become great lessons), and with rewards so great (a Luckie life), why wouldn't you want to give it a real shot? Each code you practice will take you a step closer to the life that you desire. It is yours for the taking, so take it.

Being Luckie is about much more than winning great things; it is about being able to give great things to the world. By implementing the codes found in this book, you will be able to achieve both. But first, it's important to get clear on what it means to you to succeed. How can you ever reach a goal that is not defined? One person's definition of success may be to be a Fortune 500 CEO, another's to become a professional athlete, and yet another's may be simply to be happy, healthy, and financially secure. For me, success is being able to do something that I enjoy that positively impacts the lives of others. Definitions of success between Luckies differ, but the drive to achieve them is a constant. What does success mean to you? (Code W: Winning Plans of Purpose can help with this if you're stuck.)

You have read this far, so I have every confidence that you are capable of taking this journey and leading the life that you desire. It is within your reach and you have the tools in hand to get there. Keep trucking, because the final destination—Luckieville—will be well worth it. What I need for you to do is stare fear in the face—tell it I sent you—and walk on by.

I'm so excited to hear your stories of triumph that are soon to come. Visit my site, www.gaynete.com, and send me a message all about it! If you enjoyed reading this book as much as I enjoyed writing it, do visit Amazon and write a review. When we work together, we all win.

May peace, love, and light be with you always. Shine bright, superstar, and I'll see you in Luckieville.

Gayneté

xox

THE LUCKIE DECREE

You thought we were done, didn't you? Because I want you to follow through, I have one more favor to ask of you: promise yourself (and me!) to apply all that you have learned. Come on, hand over heart (so you can feel your purpose), and repeat after me:

I will begin accepting the good things that come my way, refuse to blame, and begin pointing the finger back at myself; only then will I begin the powerful process of character building.

I will remember to dress for the success I seek, eliminate the negativity in my life, and free myself from the pesky burden of mind clutter. Oh, what a joyous day it will be when this occurs.

Giving graciously will become second nature, just like the hobby I will soon master, and my daily practice of indebtedness (gratitude) will shape my world almost instantly. Through it all, I will remember to embrace life's funnier moments. Knowing that the joke is on me will help me deal with the tougher moments that are bound to creep in from time to time, such as if I find I must let go of a relationship that no longer serves me—after all, this thing called life is famous for throwing curveballs. No matter, though, because I am a master catcher!

Above all, I will forever listen to my heart. The mentor I find and the network I develop will be like-minded individuals who follow their gut feelings the same way I do. I own my truth and stand confident knowing that there is no one out there like me; I am truly special. Prayer and questioning myself daily will keep me grounded, so I will be sure to do this.

Because I know Luckieville does not come without effort, I am willing to roll up my sleeves and get to work. Surrounding myself in solitude daily will assist me in my endeavors. The time is now to cut fear and chase my dreams, and I am ready. I will use my resources and keep a victory perspective at all times. My winning plan of purpose will keep me focused as I eliminate the hurdles that arise. With all that I set out to do, I will not be afraid of saying no, because I know a yes man becomes a trash can.

When I arrive in Luckieville, I will remain humble, because I know a "zero to hero" mentality will not serve me there.

RESOURCES: BECAUSE SHARING IS CARING!

Note: I have not been paid by any of these sites to share their information with you. In fact, they don't even know. I want you to walk away from this book with the confidence that you can live a Luckie life, and these resources will help!

Websites I Adore

www.ted.com

Ted Talks are simply amazing and uplifting. There are tons; shuffle through and find a topic that interests you.

www.google.com

This is a no-brainer, but I've decided to add it anyway. Use Google to find workshops and events where you can network and learn what you need to in order to improve your character, master your hobby, or get educated on a particular topic. Anyone can post online, however, so do use common sense when deciding to purchase something.

You can also use Google to find additional resources, such as affirmations, to assist you with areas in your life where you feel you are struggling.

www.louisehay.com/affirmations

This site provides affirmations broken down into topics ranging from forgiveness and health to prosperity and self-esteem.

Choose one that resonates with you and get to reading it daily.

www.youtube.com

Want to learn something new? Guaranteed there is a video on YouTube about it. If there isn't, you may have found a niche and can create your own YouTube videos.

www.rachelluna.biz

Rachel Luna is a confidence coach and best-selling author who can help you find the clarity you need on your road to success. She's amazing to work with and an awesome tool for your arsenal. I joined her La Plume Society (a writer's mastermind) and have enjoyed every moment.

Books That Have Helped Me on My Road to Luckieville

The Alchemist by Paulo Coelho

A novel that changed my life. A must read for anyone seeking to find their purpose in life.

What I Know for Sure by Oprah Winfrey

I read this entire book on a single plane ride—it is that good. It provides endless wisdom and amazing takeaways to be a better version of yourself.

Rich Dad Poor Dad by Robert Kiyosaki

This book tackles many of the limiting beliefs we have surrounding money and how to overcome them.

My Own Website and More

Don't forget to check out:

www.gaynete.com, www.facebook.com/gaynete, and @goalchasersclub on Instagram for motivation to assist you on your road to Luckieville. There will also be cool giveaways from time to time... because after all, sharing is caring!

Printed in Great Britain
by Amazon.co.uk, Ltd.,
Marston Gate.